International Trade and Domestic Prosperity:
Canada 1926–38

R. W. THOMPSON

International Trade
and Domestic Prosperity:
Canada 1926–38

UNIVERSITY OF TORONTO PRESS

© University of Toronto Press 1970
Printed in Great Britain for
University of Toronto Press, Toronto and Buffalo
ISBN 0-8020-1647-2

To Dorothy, Susan, and David

Acknowledgments

The enterprise from which this book has emerged has had a very long life and during this extended period I have accumulated obligations of gratitude to many individuals and to several institutions. I very deeply appreciate the advice and assistance which I have received from a large number of people, but it seems, on the whole, best not to implicate these helpful friends by name.

I have had generous financial aid from my own institution, McMaster University, from the Institute for Economic Research at Queen's University, and from the Canada Council. I should like to express my gratitude for the support which I have received from these bodies.

This work has been published with the help of a grant from the Social Science Research Council of Canada, using funds provided by the Canada Council.

Contents

Tables

International Trade and Domestic Prosperity:
Canada 1926–38

1
Introduction and Hypothesis

This study is concerned with the relationship between the balance of payments and the national income of a dependent economy. It deals, specifically, with Canadian experience in the latter part of the interwar period, but it is hoped that it will be found to have relevance to more recent events. In this first chapter there is developed a general hypothesis concerning the causes of fluctuations in national income in a dependent economy and the role of the balance of payments in relation to such fluctuations. The second chapter is devoted to establishing that the Canadian economy of the period 1926–38 was a dependent economy which was rich in natural resources and Chapter 3, to assessing the severity in Canada of the depression of the 1930s. The following three chapters are concerned with testing the hypothesis of the first chapter with reference to Canadian experience in the period 1926–38. The concluding section (Chapters 7–8) draws together the results of the empirical investigation and suggests some of their implications for economic policy.

Our first interest is, then, to develop an hypothesis concerning the causes of cyclical fluctuations in a dependent economy, but we cannot do this until the characteristics of such an economy have been outlined. The essential features of a dependent economy would appear to be two. First, an economy which fits this classification depends to an important degree on other economies both for markets and for the goods and services which its residents wish to purchase, but which it either does not produce at all or does not produce in sufficient quantities to satisfy the domestic demand. Thus, the first characteristic of a dependent economy is that its external trade is important in relation to its total economic activity. Second, the trade of the dependent economy is a small part of total world trade; more precisely, the *fluctuations* in the trade of the dependent economy are small compared with the *fluctuations* in world trade. Thus, the dependent economy is greatly influenced by the trade of other countries but has relatively little effect on the aggregate of their trade.

We wish to develop an hypothesis which will explain the cyclical fluctuations in national income in such an economy. Such fluctuations may originate either within the dependent economy, which we shall call country A, or they may be caused by forces which have their origin outside its borders. We begin by considering the first of these two possibilities.

We assume, in this first case, that there is a cyclical decline in effective demand arising from causes that are internal to country A, for example, the completion of a housing construction programme. An analysis of the situation so created suggests that no serious or protracted decline in activity in A is likely to ensue. In the first place there has been, by assumption, no change in the demand for A's exports in other countries. Since exports are an important source of income, and so of effective demand, in A they will be a major factor tending to maintain incomes there. A second factor which will help to maintain the levelof in comes in A is the improved position of A's goods in external markets. As domestic demand falls off in A some decline in domestic prices in A relative to prices in the rest of the world is likely to occur and consequently both the volume and the value of A's exports would be expected to increase. This latter statement is true on the assumptions, first that it is physically possible for A to increase her exports and, second, that the price elasticity of demand for A's exports is, in the aggregate, greater than unity.

Both of these assumptions seem likely to be valid. With respect to the first, it is difficult to conceive of any general decline in domestic demand in A (with its heavy dependence on exports) if there were no idle capacity in the export industries. If the export industries were operating at capacity output it would be almost inevitable that prosperity would be general throughout the economy, that business expectations would be favourable, and that investment would be at a high level. It would seem safe to assume that a general decline in domestic demand would be unlikely to occur if the export industries were producing at the limit of their capacity. Moreover, the very fact of the decline in domestic demand would release factors which, provided there were mobility, could be employed in increasing the output of the export industries.

The second assumption, that the price elasticity of demand for A's exports is greater than unity, seems almost certain to be valid for a dependent economy. It is possible for a single commodity that the attempt to sell a larger quantity of it would lead to such a sharp fall in its price that the total revenue from its sale would fall. If A were the only supplier of such a commodity (or if she supplied a very high proportion of world demand for such a commodity), and if most of her exports were of this type, it would follow that, as the volume of her exports increased in response to a fall in their relative prices, it would be possible for the purchasing power of A's export income to decline. But A is a small country (in the economic sense) relative to the rest of the world, and she is unlikely to be the sole or even the major supplier of most of the goods she exports. In fact, what is likely to happen in most such cases is that the prices of the goods exported by A will be set in the world market and that, except in those special cases where she supplies a very large proportion of the world market, exports from A will have a small (or even a quite negligible) effect on the world price. Thus, as relative costs fall in A because of the decline in domestic demand, the export market becomes more attractive and so A will tend to supply a somewhat larger share of it. We conclude that, except under very special circumstances, the effect of a decrease in domestic demand in A, or the assumption of no change in export demand, will tend to cause an increase in both the value and the volume of her exports.

Some of the decline in domestic demand in A will be reflected in reduced spending on imports; and the more severe the decline in total spending the greater the decline in spending on imports may be expected to be. As resources become unemployed in A, the position of the import-competing industries in A will be strengthened both because costs in A are likely to fall relative to costs abroad and also because the decline in domestic prices relative to prices abroad may have some effect in inducing consumers to allocate a rather larger proportion of their spending to home-produced goods which may not compete directly with imports.

The decline in domestic demand is, therefore, likely to strengthen A's balance of payments on current account and this will tend to offset in some measure the effects of that decline in demand. If it were considered desirable to adopt, in addition, a policy designed to encourage internal expansion, the strengthened position of the balance of payments would make it easier to give effect to such a policy. But, quite apart from any deliberate expansionist policy, the operation of free market forces would have an effect in offsetting the initial decline in domestic demand. And since, by definition, foreign trade is important to A, the effect of such forces would be correspondingly great.

It is possible that the strengthened position of A's current account balance of payments would lead to an appreciation of A's currency in the foreign exchange market. This might partially offset the effect of the relative reduction in prices in A but could not do so entirely so long as economic activity in A remained below its initial level, since it is the decline from this initial level which is responsible for the improved balance of payments. There is, in fact, no necessity for any appreciation in the external value of A's currency; any surplus could be lent abroad or it could be used to repay former borrowings. For our present purposes the conclusion from this analysis is that a serious cyclical depression is unlikely to be generated in A by internal forces alone.

If serious depressions are not generated within country A and if A is subject to such disturbances, they must be transmitted to A from abroad. There would seem to be three channels through which such disturbances could be transmitted to A, viz., the current account of the balance of payments, the capital account, and psychological influences. These three categories would appear to be exhaustive.[1]

We shall deal first with psychological influences or changes in expectations. In considering this question we must recognize that there may be a change in expectations either within A or outside of A. If the change in expectations occurs within A, it is an internal influence and as such is unlikely to cause a major cyclical disturbance in A for reasons which were discussed above. If there is a change in expectations outside of A and this change is communicated to A through channels other than her transactions with other countries, for example, through personal contacts or newspapers, there will be a change in internal expectations. This case was discussed above. If the change in expectations abroad is not communicated through some such means as those indicated and if it does not affect transactions with other countries, there will be no effect on A.

Finally, the change in expectations abroad may affect A's transactions with other countries. In this case the impact of the change in expectations abroad is felt in A only because it affects her balance of payments. We conclude that a change in expectations in A can be treated as an internal factor and so will be unlikely to generate a major cyclical disturbance, and that a change in expectations abroad becomes significant to A only through its effect on her balance of payments.

It is clear that the next phase of this analysis must consider the possibility of cyclical disturbances being transmitted to A through her balance of payments. We assume, as above, that the world consists, on the one hand, of our dependent economy, A, and, on the other hand, of the rest of the world, B. We are concerned only with the effects of the various changes on A, conditions in B being of interest to us only in so far as they affect A. We assume that initially the economy of A is in equilibrium in the sense that there is no tendency toward a change in the level of domestic activity there or in her balance of payments; there may be, but there is not necessarily, full employment.

We consider first the possibility that cyclical disturbances are communicated to A through the current account of her balance of payments. In order to isolate the effects of changes in A's current account balance, we shall assume in this part of the analysis that initially A's current account credits are just equal to her current account debits, that A has no other external transactions, and that any transactions other than those on current account that may subsequently arise are merely of an accommodating nature, induced by changes in the current account.

Suppose that, under the conditions assumed in the preceding paragraph, a depression develops in B. Income in B will then be lower because of the depression and consequently there will be a decline in spending in B. This decline in spending implies a reduction in demand in B both for domestic goods and for imports, i.e., there will be a decline in B's demand for A's goods.[2] This will lead to a fall in both the price and the volume of A's exports.

Since both the quantity and the price of A's exports have fallen, there will be a fall in the real incomes of exporters in A. As a result, the suppliers of factors to A's export industries will find that their incomes have fallen because of the decline in export demand. Since their incomes will now be lower, these factor suppliers will reduce their spending. But exports are, by definition, an important source of income in A and so the effects of the reduction in exports will spread throughout A's economy. The lower level of employment and income will cause a reduction in A's demand for imports.[3] The obverse of this is, of course, a decline in B's exports but, since A is such a small country while B represents the rest of the world, the effects in B on such measures as aggregate income and employment are likely to be relatively very small.

Thus, in this case, the effects of the depression which originate in B are transferred to A through a decline in her exports, which leads to a general decline in income and so to a decline in imports into A. A new equilibrium will not be established until the balance on current account in one direction is just offset by an autonomous capital movement of equal magnitude in the other direction.

The current account of the balance of payments thus appears to provide a mechanism by which cyclical disturbances may be introduced into a dependent economy, but this is not necessarily the only vehicle of transmission. We must now consider the possibility that cyclical disturbances may be transmitted to A through the capital account of her balance of payments.

When we consider the transactions on capital account of a dependent country with the rest of the world, it is convenient to distinguish two types of dependent countries. First, there are the older and economically more developed countries. In such economies the natural resources will have been exploited to an extent comparable with that in major mature industrial economies. The second group of dependent countries we can characterize as the "resource economies." These are the relatively undeveloped economies which have unexplored frontiers in the economic, and possibly also in the geographic, sense. Such countries are almost certain to be net debtors on international capital account – they will have borrowed abroad to cover a part, at least, of the cost of developing their resources and will not yet have repaid all of these borrowings. To consider fully the possible role of capital account transactions in transmitting cycles to these two types of dependent economies would require two separate analyses; but the empirical parts of this study are concerned with the Canadian economy in the interwar period and it will be sufficient to develop the analysis for the dependent resource economy only because, as is shown in Chapter 2, this is the group to which Canada belonged in the period under consideration.

Certain general characteristics of such economies are worth mentioning because an awareness of them will facilitate the subsequent analysis. These resource economies will have a relatively high ratio of natural resources relative to the population and, *a fortiori*, as comparatively undeveloped countries, they would be expected to have a relatively high ratio of *undeveloped* resources relative to the population. This comparative abundance of natural resources implies a high standard of living, but if institutional factors are unfavourable it may not be realized. Finally, such resource economies are almost certain to be exporters of the products of the extractive industries in raw or, in some cases, in manufactured form, and to be importers of those types of manufactured products which can be produced most economically in a more fully industrialized economy; in particular, the dependent economy is likely to be heavily dependent on other countries for complex manufactured goods such as industrial machinery and similar equipment.[4]

We wish to consider the possible role of the capital account of the balance of payments in transmitting cycles to such a dependent resource economy. It would be possible to carry out an analysis for the capital account of the balance of payments which would parallel the analysis we have made for the current account. Such an analysis would treat changes in the capital account as autonomous and all changes in the current account as accommodating changes. This analysis would be not only highly abstract but, if considered in isolation, would be found to contribute little of a positive character to the formulation of our hypothesis. It seems more appropriate (and it will certainly be less tedious) to proceed directly to a consideration of the more plausible case in which both the current account and the capital account can play active roles in the transmission of cyclical disturbances. The hypothesis which is developed below considers the causal sequence of events; this may be (but will not necessarily be) their chronological order.

1 We begin from a position of equilibrium in both A and B. In each there is assumed to be a reasonable measure of prosperity, but there is not necessarily full employment. Since A is a resource economy, there will be relatively more unexploited investment opportunities in A than in B; and the prevalence of prosperity will create conditions favourable to the rapid development of A's resources. In such circumstances it is probable that domestic savings in A will be insufficient to finance the desired volume of investment in that country and that the deficiency will be made up by borrowing from B. Because A has large unexploited resources

which, in a period of prosperity, would offer favourable opportunities for investment, it seems likely that lenders in B will be as anxious to lend as borrowers in A will be to borrow.[5] Now a considerable part of the resources required for investment cannot by their very nature be imported and so we would expect that, to some considerable degree, A will import consumption goods in order to release her domestic resources to produce, for the investment industries, goods and services which it is either impossible or impracticable to import. Thus, notwithstanding the likelihood, as we have noted above, that A will be an importer of complex manufactured capital goods, we would not be surprised to find a larger proportion of A's resources than of B's employed in the capital goods industries, especially in construction, where a large proportion of the resources must be provided at the site.

2   We assume that, beginning from the position described above, a downturn occurs in B. This implies a reduction in output, employment, and income. There will probably also be a decline in the price level in B relative to that in A because of the decline in aggregate demand in B.

3   As a result of the downturn in B there will be some reduction in B's spending on domestic goods and also on imports from A (assuming that A's exports are not, in the aggregate, inferior goods).

4   These developments imply a decline in the real incomes of the owners of factors of production employed in the export industries in A. Since the export industries in A are an important part of her economy, any major decline in exports will represent, in itself, an appreciable decline in total income.

5   Reduced incomes in the export industries will cause reduced spending by those who derive income from such industries and so the decline in export incomes will spread to the domestic industries in A. And again, because of the importance of exports to A's economy, any serious decline in incomes and spending in her export industries will represent a serious decline in demand for those industries which supply domestic demand. Thus the depression in A's export industries will spread to her domestic industries and so the ramifications will be felt throughout the economy.

6   The reduced demand for A's goods both at home and abroad implies unused capacity in both the domestic and the export industries in A. There will be (apart from special cases) no need for any net increase in productive facilities. Consequently, there will be a fall in investment in A. The direct effects of the decline in all of the major components of demand (except, possibly, for that which originates in spending by governments) and the indirect effect through the decline in profits that will ensue will cause business expectations to become unfavourable.[6] In such circumstances "present fears are less than horrible imaginings" and investment will decline further.

7   Two related results of the decline in investment in A may be noted:

(a) Since investment was relatively more important in A than in B in the period of prosperity, the effect of the fall in investment will have more serious consequences for A. To some extent the effects of the relatively sharper fall in investment in A will be cushioned by the improvement in her balance of payments on current account. To the extent that A's factors are mobile, some of those which were employed in the capital goods industries may return to producing consumer goods and, if this happens, it will cause some further improvement in A's balance of payments.

(b) The lower level of investment in A brings with it reduced dependence on borrowed capital because domestic savings will be more nearly adequate to (and may even exceed) the requirements for investment under the conditions of depression which now exist in A.[7] This reduction in capital inflows is, of course, the obverse of the changes in the current account referred to in (a) above.

8   Because incomes and investment in A have fallen, exports from B to A will be reduced. But, since A is a small economy compared with B, the effects of the depression in A on the level of aggregate income and employment in B will be minor. No serious error is introduced into our analysis by ignoring any subsequent effects on A's exports and income caused by the decline in B's incomes resulting from reduced exports from B to A, i.e., by ignoring the foreign repercussions of developments in A, since A is, by definition, a small country (in the economic sense) compared with B.

9   The recovery of A from the depression depends upon recovery in B since, for reasons which were discussed above, recovery cannot proceed very far in a dependent economy unless there is also recovery in the rest of the world.

10   Eventually there will be a revival of economic activity in B and the whole process described above will be reversed. Increased activity and spending in B will bring about an increase in the volume and, probably, in the prices of imports from A. Incomes will increase in A's export industries and the increased spending which results will raise incomes in the domestic sectors of A's economy. As both exports and domestic demand increase, some industries will find themselves approaching capacity output. If, as is possible in such circumstances, prices increase more rapidly than average costs, profits will be higher both because of the increased profit per unit of production and because of the increased quantity of product which is being sold. Thus investment in both domestic and in export industries will increase. Expectations will almost certainly become favourable if the market for exports continues to improve. If these trends persist, the rate at which it will be desired to develop A's resources will be expected, sooner or later, to exceed that which could be financed from domestic savings. Capital from B will flow to A in response to the demand of borrowers in A and because lenders in B will feel that investment opportunities in A are such as to offer attractive outlets for some of their capital. And so the cycle will be completed.

The general hypothesis developed above to explain the cycle in a dependent resource economy appears to meet the preliminary test of providing an internally consistent explanation of the business cycle in such an economy. In succeeding chapters this initial hypothesis will be tested in relation to the facts as they were experienced in Canada in the years 1926–38.

2
Canada as a Dependent Resource Economy

The hypothesis which has been developed in the first chapter applies to a dependent resource economy. We wish to examine this hypothesis further in relation to the Canadian experience in the period 1926–38, but it is necessary first to establish that the Canadian economy of that period had the characteristics of a dependent resource economy as defined in Chapter 1.

The economy with which our hypothesis is concerned has, as explained in Chapter 1, three characteristics. First, the external trade of such an economy is important in relation to its aggregate economic activity. Since this study is concerned with cyclical behaviour we are, in fact, more interested in the *changes* in the total value of external trade (and more especially in exports) in relation to *changes* in the size of the national income than in comparing the two aggregates, i.e., it is the marginal rather than the average ratio of exports to income that is of primary interest. Second, the external trade of the economy is a small proportion of total world trade or, more relevantly in the present case, *fluctuations* in the external trade of the dependent economy are a small fraction of *fluctuations* in total world trade. Third, the country has a high ratio of natural resources, and especially of undeveloped natural resources, to population. We shall examine these three questions in turn in order to show that, for the period with which this study deals, the Canadian economy had the three characteristics of a dependent resource economy as that term is used here.

It may be well, at the outset, to be more specific about the conditions which must be satisfied for an economy to be a "dependent resource economy" in the present context. The hypothesis of Chapter 1 was developed by considering a dependent resource economy, A, on the one hand, in relation to the rest of the world, B, on the other. It is necessary to show only that, if our hypothesis is to apply, Canada had the characteristics of A. In order to be a dependent economy, as we use the term, it is necessary that Canada be dependent in relation to the rest of the world, i.e., that economic activity in Canada be greatly affected by events in the rest of the world, and that the rest of the world be affected only slightly by events in Canada. There is, theoretically, no reason why each separate country, taken by itself, could not be dependent in relation to all other countries taken together. The obvious analogy is to the individual firm in an industry in which there are many firms; the individual firm may have a negligible influence on the industry but be itself greatly affected by changes which affect the industry as a whole.

Although it is theoretically possible for all economies to be "dependent," it is not even theoretically possible for all to be "resource" economies as the term is used here. Country A is here considered to have a resource economy only if it has a high ratio of natural resources to population *compared with the ratio in the rest of the world*. Then, under conditions of general prosperity, A should be able, *ceteris paribus*, to compete successfully for the net capital imports it requires if it is to develop its resources more rapidly than would be possible with capital from domestic sources alone. Consequently, it is necessary to make a comparison with other countries, either individually or in the aggregate, to establish that A has a resource economy; it is not necessary to make such a comparison to establish that A has a dependent economy.

The first question we have to consider is the magnitude of Canada's external trade in relation to some measure of her national income. One of the assumptions made to develop the hypothesis of Chapter 1 was that external trade, and especially changes in the receipts from sales abroad of goods and services, played an important role in the explanation of the cyclical fluctuations in national income of a dependent resource economy. Our primary purpose here is to show that, for Canada in the period 1926–38, fluctuations in total current account credits were important relative to fluctuations in national income. In order to do this, we shall establish that total exports were important relative to total national income, and from this it will be possible to reach a conclusion concerning the order of magnitude of the ratio of *changes* in current account credits to *changes* in national income.

As the measure of external trade we use total current account credits, i.e., the total value of exports of goods and services as these are shown in the published statements of the Canadian balance of international payments.[1] Exports are used in preference to imports because of the greater emphasis placed on the role of exports in the first chapter. It would, of course, be possible to consider both exports and imports but, since the two were very nearly equal for the period as a whole, we shall concentrate our attention in this chapter on exports.[2]

The most appropriate measure of national income for our purpose is the Gross National Expenditure. This is the measure of aggregate income which will be used in subsequent chapters and it is convenient to use the same measure here. In addition, exports are one component of Gross National Expenditure (hereafter abbreviated to GNE) and, since we are interested in the ratio of exports to national income, it is desirable to use measures of the two magnitudes which are directly comparable. The data for the GNE are readily available from the *National Accounts*.[3]

The period with which we are dealing covers the thirteen years from 1926 to 1938 inclusive. For purposes of the present chapter and, more specifically, for purposes of the first two of the three points which are examined in it, figures will be given for the four representative years 1928, 1932, 1935, and 1938. These years are well spaced through the period and are representative also of the varying degrees of prosperity and depression (with their implications for income and external trade) which were experienced in this period. If we can establish that the Canadian economy had the required attributes for these four years, it can safely be assumed that they were present in the other years of the period.

Table I provides the statistics to show that external trade was important in relation to national income in Canada. The upper section of this table shows exports of commodities plus services at current prices as percentages of GNE in each of the four years. The lower section of the table shows the corresponding statistics when the two measures are valued at constant (1935–9 average) prices.

The value of exports of goods and services measured in terms of current prices did not fall as low as 20 per cent, nor did it rise as high as 30 per cent of GNE in any of the years shown in Table I. The average for the four years is 25 per cent. When both exports and GNE are valued at constant (1935–9) prices the average ratio of exports to GNE is not materially affected; it increases slightly to 26 per cent compared with the figure of 25 per cent when current values are used. The range of the percentage figures is considerably narrowed, however, when constant prices are used, and in this case the ratio varies within the much narrower range of 25–7 per cent. The reason for this narrowing of the range is to be found in the sharper

TABLE I
VALUE OF EXPORTS AND GROSS NATIONAL EXPENDITURE

	1928	1932	1935	1938
(a) Current dollars				
Total exports of goods and services (millions)	1,788	808	1,139*	1,351*
Gross National Expenditure (millions)	6,046	3,827	4,315	5,278
Total exports of goods and services as percentage of GNE	29%	21%	26%	26%
(b) Constant (1935–9) dollars				
Total exports of goods and services (millions)	1,425	979	1,204	1,346
Gross National Expenditure (millions)	5,295	3,910	4,473	5,106
Total exports of goods and services as percentage of GNE	27%	25%	27%	26%

*These figures are $6 million below the official balance of payments figures for 1935 and $10 million below those for 1938. The adjustment in the official figures was made to achieve consistency in the treatment of revenues from freight and shipping services in those years compared with the earlier years of the period. For further explanation, see Chapters 4 and 5.

Sources: Canada, Dominion Bureau of Statistics, *National Accounts, Income and Expenditures 1926–56* (Ottawa 1958), 32, Table II, and *The Canadian Balance of International Payments, 1926 to 1948* (Ottawa 1949), 154, 158.
Statistics used in (b) above are based on calculations made for Chapters 4 and 6 of this study.

decline in export prices than in the general price level in Canada between 1928 and 1932. When the effects of this are removed from the two series by valuing each at constant prices, the fluctuations in the ratio are, of course, reduced. The most important fact which is brought out in Table I is that, on the average, exports of goods and services were very close to 25 per cent of GNE whether the figures are based on current or constant prices.

These figures establish the fact that exports were a large component of national income, but such figures understate the real importance of exports in the Canadian economy. It is true that about one-quarter of GNE arose directly as the proceeds of sales of goods and services abroad, but, in addition, a substantial fraction of domestic expenditures was dependent upon conditions in the export industries. It is immediately obvious, for example, that the sales of enterprises concerned with supplying the domestic market in such export areas as the wheat-growing sections of the prairie provinces, the pulp and paper-producing towns, or the mining communities across the country were directly related to the fortunes of the producers of the basic export commodities. It is not necessary here to attempt to pursue further or to make a statistical estimate of these indirect effects. For our present purposes it is sufficient to show that the income which was derived directly from exports was a major component of total GNE and that its importance would be considerably increased if we were to make allowance for only the most direct and obvious secondary effects.[4]

This analysis shows that exports were important as a source of income, both directly and indirectly; but we are concerned principally with *changes* in economic magnitudes, and so it is the marginal ratio of exports to GNE that has greater relevance for our purposes. The ratio of changes in current account credits to changes in GNE can be computed for six time periods from the data in Table I. The results of these calculations are shown in Table II.

TABLE II
CHANGES IN CANADA'S CURRENT ACCOUNT CREDITS AS PERCENTAGE OF CHANGES IN GNE

Period	Percentage computed from current dollar values	Percentage computed from values at 1935–9 prices
1928–32	44	32
1928–35	37	27
1928–38	57	42
1932–5	68	40
1932–8	37	31
1935–8	22	22
Mean	44	32

Source: Calculated from data in Table I.

It is evident from the figures in this table that the marginal ratio of exports to GNE is typically somewhat higher than the average ratio. The mean of the six observations when the magnitudes are valued at current prices is 44 per cent; on the basis of 1935–9 prices it is 32 per cent. The corresponding figures for the average ratio are 25 and 26 per cent respectively. The marginal ratio was not less than 22 per cent in any of the six periods. The most significant conclusion which we derive from these calculations is that, on the average, the marginal ratio of the value of exports of goods and services to GNE was approximately one-third when both measures are valued at average 1935–9 prices; and it is the ratio in terms of constant prices which is more relevant for our purposes.

In the case of the marginal ratio, as in the case of the average ratio, the calculation described above understates the relative importance of fluctuations in the value of exports because changes in the value of exports would lead to similar changes in the same direction in domestic expenditures in those regions of the economy which are heavily dependent upon exports. If both current account credits and GNE are measured at constant prices, it was concluded above that changes in the former measure were, on the average, about one-third of changes in GNE. This proportion would be considerably greater if allowance were made for only those changes in domestic expenditure which were direct consequences of the changes in the value of exports.

Another way of viewing the importance of exports in relation to national income is to compare the proportion of Canada with that for a number of other countries. In a strict sense, as pointed out earlier, this comparison is not germane to the present inquiry. We are concerned with establishing that the fluctuations in exports were important in their influence on fluctuations in GNE in Canada, and this is independent of the experience of other individual countries. But if there are economies which are dependent in this respect, and if the ratio for Canada is high in comparison with most other economies, this suggests, although it does not prove, that Canada was also a dependent economy.

For the prewar years, reasonably adequate national income figures are available for a relatively small number of countries. The number for which we have comprehensive statistics of trade in services as well as in goods is even smaller. In Table III,

TABLE III
CURRENT ACCOUNT CREDITS AS A PERCENTAGE OF NATIONAL INCOME
FOR SELECTED COUNTRIES, SELECTED YEARS

	1928	1932	1935	1938	Average percentage for years shown
United States of America	8	5	5	6	6
United Kingdom	29	16	18	15	20
France	24	8	8	5	11
Netherlands	—*	28	26	20	24
New Zealand	31	24	23	20	24
Union of South Africa	29	28	32	34	31
Canada†	35	27	32	31	31

*Data concerning balance of payments not available for 1928.
†The figures shown here differ from those in Table I because it was necessary in this table to make the Canadian figures comparable with those for the other countries. Limitations in data available made it impossible to prepare figures for the other countries shown in this table on the same basis as that used for Canada in Table I. The general conclusions to be drawn are not materially affected by these limitations in the data.

Sources: League of Nations, *Balances of Payments,* various years (Geneva). Colin Clark, *Conditions of Economic Progress,* 3rd ed. (Macmillan and Co. 1957), Ch. III.

the ratio of total current account credits to net national income at factor cost in 1928, 1932, 1935, and 1938 is given for those countries for which data could be obtained.[5]

This table shows that, taking the average of the four years, exports were more important in relation to national income for Canada than for any of the other countries for which data could be obtained except, possibly, South Africa. It will be noted that, for the four countries at the bottom of the table, the proportion of exports to national income was greater than for the other three. Of these four countries, South Africa and New Zealand may be classed, in terms of the criteria we are using here, along with Canada as dependent resource economies. The Netherlands would also be classed as a dependent economy, but it differs from the other three countries mentioned in that it has a much lower ratio of natural resources to population, i.e., the Netherlands is a dependent economy, but it is not a resource economy.

We are interested also in the marginal ratio of the value of current account credits to GNE. Examination of the cyclical behaviour of the average ratios for the different countries makes it at once apparent that the marginal ratio for Canada was, on the average, higher than for any of the other countries for which data are given in Table III.

The second point which we wish to establish in this chapter is that Canada's trade, and the fluctuations in it, were a small fraction of world trade, and fluctuations in it. Here, again, our primary interest is with trade in goods and services and not only with commodity trade. The figures for Canada's trade in goods and services for the four selected years have been presented in Table I. The other figures required are those for total world trade in goods and services for the same four years. These figures are shown in Table IV; their derivation is explained in Appendix B.

TABLE IV
CANADIAN AND WORLD TRADE IN GOODS AND SERVICES (in billions of US current dollars)

	1928	1932	1935	1938
Merchandise trade (excluding newly-mined gold and silver)	32·6	12·9	19·0	21·9
Newly-mined gold	1·2	1·8*	4·1	3·2
Newly-mined silver	0·3	0·5*	0·5	0·3
Freight and shipping, etc.	2·9	1·1	2·0	2·7
Tourist and travel	1·4	0·5	0·5	0·6*
Interest and dividends	2·8	1·2	1·8	2·0*
Emigrants' remittances	0·4	0·2	0·1	0·1*
Total above	41·6	18·2	28·0	30·8
US dollar equivalent of Canadian current account credits	1·8	0·7	1·1	1·3
Current account credits of world excluding Canada	39·8	17·5	26·9	29·5
Canadian current account credits as percentage of rest of the world	4·5%	4·0%	4·1%	4·4%

*World total estimated on basis of percentage change for major countries.

Sources: League of Nations, *The Network of World Trade* (Geneva 1942), Annex I, 100 and Annex II, 103; *Balances of Payments*, various years; *Review of World Trade, 1934*.

Two comments are required in connection with this table. The first is that it is obvious from the last line that Canada's trade in goods and services was a small percentage of world trade. It was, indeed, somewhat smaller than indicated by this table since the coverage of the figures for Canada is relatively more complete than is that of the figures we have been able to obtain, especially for services, for the world as a whole.

The second comment is concerned with the fluctuations in Canadian trade in relation to world trade. From the figures for the four years it is possible to calculate the ratio of changes in Canada's trade to fluctuations in the trade (in both goods and services) of the rest of the world for six time periods as shown in Table v. This ratio varied within the range 4·3 to 5·3 per cent except for the relatively brief 1935–8 period when it was 8·1 per cent. In general, it seems fair to say that for this period the fluctuations in Canada's exports of goods and services were approximately 5 per cent of the figure for the rest of the world.

The figures which we have been considering are expressed in current dollars of the respective years, but for most purposes in this study values are measured in

TABLE V
FLUCTUATIONS IN CANADA'S TRADE IN GOODS AND SERVICES AS
A PERCENTAGE OF FLUCTUATIONS IN REST OF WORLD

	Change in rest of world exports (billions of US dollars)	Change in Canada's exports* (millions of US dollars)	Canadian fluctuations as percentage of fluctuations in rest of world†
1928–32	$22·3	$1,075	4·8
1928–35	12·9	653	5·1
1928–38	10·3	443	4·3
1932–5	9·4	422	4·5
1932–8	12·0	632	5·3
1935–8	2·6	210	8·1

*These figures were derived from those calculated for Table IV before the latter were rounded.
†Value of Canadian trade and value of world trade fluctuated in the same direction in each period, and therefore the signs in this column are all positive.

Source: Table IV.

constant dollars. In the present context a case could be made for either measure and so we shall attempt to estimate what the ratios would be if the value were measured in constant prices. This calculation, which can be only a rough approximation because of limitations in the data available,[6] indicates that Canada's current account credits when valued at constant (1928) prices varied between 4 and 6 per cent of the total for the rest of the world. The average for the period as a whole was just under 5 per cent. The corresponding marginal ratio, as nearly as we can determine it from the data available, appears to have been between 6 and 7 per cent.

In this section, despite the limitations in some of the data, we have been able to establish with sufficient accuracy for our purposes that, whether the values are measured at current or at constant prices, Canadian current account credits and fluctuations in them were a small percentage of the comparable magnitudes for the rest of the world. And this general conclusion, unsatisfactory as it is from the viewpoint of precise numerical measurement, is sufficient for our present purposes.

The third and final point to establish is that Canada was, in the period 1926–38, a resource economy in the sense in which that term was used in Chapter 1. The problem here is rather more nebulous than were the two others examined in this chapter, and just how to deal with it is by no means obvious. One possibility is to say that "everyone knows" that Canada was, and still is, a country rich in natural resources, many of which have not been by any means fully developed; and what is true today was true a fortiori in the earlier period with which this study deals.[7]

The mere fact that something is widely assumed to be true does not necessarily mean that it is true; there are numerous instances of propositions whose truth has long been widely accepted and which have subsequently been shown to be incorrect. Such propositions have usually been concerned with matters more abstract than the question at issue here. Whether or not a country is rich in natural resources would appear to be a rather basic question, and if the popular assumption that the country has such resources is maintained over a long period of time, as it has been in this case, we may accept this as substantial evidence in support of the truth of the proposition. But, regardless of how widely and persistently held or how soundly based this viewpoint may be, it does not provide a very scientific background for this

TABLE VI
NATIONAL RESOURCES PER HEAD OF POPULATION

	Coal and lignite reserves coal equivalent (tons/head)	Potential water power at ordinary min flow (H.P./head)	Iron ore metal content (tons/head)	Arable and other cultivated land (acres/head)	Pasture (acres/head)
United Kingdom	3,700	0·015	38·1	0·28	0·40
West Continental Europe	1,510	0·20	31·4	1·09	0·47
East Continental Europe	980	0·10	4·1	1·34	0·51
USSR	6,300	0·46	94·0	2·35	5·70
USA and Cuba	17,000	0·25	48·0	2·66	4·40
Canada and Newfoundland	37,300	2·27	217·1	5·04	6·78
South Africa	20,600	0·23	300·0	1·31	10·00
Australia and New Zealand	3,580	0·64	20·7	3·74	17·00
Argentina, Uruguay, Chile	107	0·48	12·7	4·64	18·70
India	66	0·10	5·9	1·29	0·52
China	546	0·05	1·4	0·55	1·78
Japan	227	0·10	0·4	0·23	0·11
All countries listed	3,000	0·16	24·6	1·30	2·10

Source: A. J. Brown, *Industrialization and Trade*, Royal Institute of International Affairs (London 1943), 21, Table II.

study. We must, therefore, examine some more concrete and quantitative measures.

By "natural resources" we mean the free gifts of nature or the agents of production which occur free in nature. The most important of these are usually considered to be those which provide energy or food and raw materials.[8] The resources which have traditionally been considered the major sources of energy are coal and water-power, petroleum and natural gas having come into greater prominence in more recent years.[9] The sources of food and raw materials are agricultural land, mines, forests, and fisheries. There are important fishing areas off both the east and west coasts of Canada (and there is also a substantial industry concerned with inland fisheries), but the vessels of several nations are found in some of the major fishing areas. We shall, therefore, note that Canada has major fishing resources and give no further consideration to this matter.

Of the remaining natural resources, those which would seem to have been of greatest importance in our period are coal and waterpower as energy sources, agricultural land as a source of food and raw materials, and iron ore which (along with coal) has provided the resource base for industrial economies. Table VI shows the position of various countries and regions with respect to these resources in the years immediately before 1939.

We see from this table that, on a per capita basis, Canada and Newfoundland ranked first among the countries shown in coal and lignite, waterpower, and arable and other cultivated land.[10] In iron ore and pasture land they ranked second and fourth, respectively. For each of the five resources, the figure for Canada and Newfoundland was at least three times as large as the average for all countries shown. This table, which, it may be relevant to mention, was not prepared with any special reference to Canada, makes it abundantly clear that the country was especially well endowed with the basic natural resources.

The principal natural resources which are not dealt with in Table VI are the metals other than iron ore, and forest products. The most important of the other metals in our period were copper, lead, zinc, nickel, tin, bauxite, and gold.[11] The principal forest products are roundwood, sawn lumber, wood pulp, chemical pulp, and newsprint.[12] Table VII shows, for each of these products, and for a few others,

TABLE VII
CANADIAN AND WORLD PRODUCTION OF IMPORTANT MINERAL AND
FOREST PRODUCTS, 1937 AND 1955

	1937			1955		
	Canada (including Newfound-land)	World	Canada as % of World	Canada (including Newfound-land)	World	Canada as % of World
Population* (millions)	11·3	2,013	0·6	16·1	2,737	0·6
Mineral products						
Gold (thousands of kilogrammes)	128	919	14	141	840	17
Silver (thousands of metric tons)	760	8,400	9	896	5,900	15
Nickel (thousands of metric tons)	102	113	90	159	205	78
Copper (thousands of metric tons)	249	2,190	11	296	2,730	11
Lead (thousands of metric tons)	216	1,640	13	184	1,930	10
Zinc (thousands of metric tons)	232	1,835	13	393	2,640	15
Tin (thousands of metric tons)	—	210	0	†	15,350	†
Bauxite (thousands of metric tons)	—	3,700	0	—	15,350	0
Asbestos (thousands of metric tons)	372	480	78	965	1,315	73
Forest products						
Roundwood (millions of cu. metres)	67·4	1,220	6	92·9	1,580	6
Lumber, sawn (millions of cu. metres)	9·4	185	5	19·8	291	7
Wood pulp (thousands of metric tons)	3,269	9,600	34	5,114	15,330	33
Chemical pulp (thousands of metric tons)	1,601	14,000	11	4,095	30,300	14
Newsprint (thousands of metric tons)	3,651	8,100	45	5,593	11,030	51

*Population figures are for 1937 and 1956.
†Less than one-half.

Source: United Nations, *Statistical Yearbook*, 1957, Forestry and Mining Statistics.

the physical volume of Canadian and world production and Canadian as a percentage of world production in 1937 and 1955.[13] It will be noted that, for all of these commodities except tin and bauxite, Canada's share of world production was much greater than her population, expressed as a percentage of world population.[14]

Table VII also shows that not only was Canada rich in natural resources in 1937, but that she had large undeveloped resources at that date, i.e., almost at the end of the period covered by this study. It will be observed, first, that for each of these commodities, with the single exception of lead, the physical volume of production in 1955 exceeded that for 1937.[15] In addition, for six of the eleven commodities which were produced in Canada, her proportion of the world total was higher in 1955 than in 1937. For three of the others the proportion was constant or changed very little. Only for three of these major commodities (nickel, asbestos, and lead) did Canada's share of world production fall by any appreciable proportion. And, in the case of both nickel and asbestos, Canada was still producing in 1955 more than 70 per cent of total world output.

We may conclude from this that in the period 1926–38 Canada had not only a high proportion of natural resources to population but that she also had abundant unexploited resources at the end of this period.

It is also relevant for our purposes to examine the behaviour of investment in the resource industries. Our hypothesis was that, in periods of general prosperity, a young country which had large undeveloped resources would tend to have a high rate of investment to develop its resources. For the resource industries we find that the capital stock (net of depreciation and valued at 1949 prices) increased in every year from 1945 to 1955, when the series ends. For 1955 the capital stock for these industries was $5·2 billion compared with $2·0 billion in 1945.[16] This is an increase of approximately 160 per cent in a ten-year period. If we take a later year as a starting point, so as to avoid the possible influence of any unusual conditions in the immediate postwar period, we find that, from 1952 to 1955, there was an increase in the capital stock (at 1949 prices) of over $1 billion or more than 25 per cent of the figure at the beginning of this shorter period.[17] The fact of this rapid increase in the physical capital stock of the resource industries in the postwar period makes it clear that there were abundant unexploited natural resources at the end of the prewar period and that, as the hypothesis suggests, these were subject to rapid development when favourable conditions appeared.

We have now established that in the period 1926–38 Canada had a high ratio of natural resources, developed and undeveloped, to population. It was shown earlier that Canada was a dependent economy from 1926 to 1938, and we have, therefore, now demonstrated that in this period Canada was a dependent resource economy as defined in Chapter 1.

3
Unemployment
in Canada, 1926–41

Our concern in this chapter, and in the related Appendix C, is to estimate the magnitude of unemployment in Canada in each of the years 1926 to 1941. The figures derived for this purpose will give a general measure of the severity of depression in each year; this measure is important in its own right and also provides a quantitative measure of the central problem of economic policy during most of the period. It provides, therefore, an essential part of the background for the analysis which will occupy most of the subsequent chapters.

We shall begin by considering which measure of unemployment is most appropriate for our purposes, and then proceed to give a general description of the methods used in making the estimates of unemployment and present the results of the calculations. The detailed statistical background and a more complete description of the procedure will be found in Appendix C.

For purposes of this study, it is desirable to measure the extent of unemployment in any year by the extent to which GNE in that year, measured at 1935–9 prices, fell short of what it would have been, also at 1935–9 prices, if there had been full employment. Since the term *unemployment* is often used to refer to the number, or the percentage, of individuals in the labour force who are unemployed, it should be explained why the GNE measure of unemployment is used here.

The first reason for preferring the GNE measure in the present study is that there seems, as a matter of economic principle, no reason for using unemployment with reference to the unemployment of individuals, i.e., of the factor labour, only. When other available factors of production are not in use, the production, and the possible consumption, of goods and services is reduced below what it might have been just as is the case when individuals are unemployed. Or, to put the same thing from a different point of view, owners of other factors which are not employed are deprived of the income they would have received just as the unemployed individual is deprived of income he would have received if his labour had been employed. A comprehensive measure of unemployment should consider the effect of the unemployment of all factors and not that of labour only.

The second reason for preferring the GNE measure is that it avoids certain statistical problems in measuring the amount of unemployment. The GNE approach takes the view that if there were full employment in any year the output of goods and services would have some aggregate value and the extent to which the actual value of production falls short of this full employment figure is the measure of unemployment in that year. If, for example, a man is working only part-time he would be classed either as employed or unemployed if one were enumerating the number of individuals who were without work. But he is obviously partially employed, and it is desirable that this partial employment be reflected in the measure of unemployment. If, in any year, there is more short time unemployment than would normally be the case at full employment, production will be reduced and such partial unemployment will be reflected directly in a reduced GNE. Again, if unemployment is measured by the total number of unemployed individuals, there is the implicit assumption that labour is homogeneous. But, if, for example, a highly skilled craftsman is unemployed, the loss of production (although not necessarily the loss of utility to the unemployed individual) is greater than if an unskilled worker is unemployed.[1] Since the purpose of economic activity is to permit people to consume rather than to provide employment, it is clearly desirable in this study to have a measure of unemployment that indicates the loss of potential output. In general, the GNE approach has the statistical advantage that it enables us to convert unemployment of whatever type into homogeneous units (dollars of 1935–9 purchasing power).[2] Thus qualitative differences are taken into account by the GNE measure which are necessarily ignored when unemployment is measured by an enumeration of the number of unemployed individuals.

A third advantage of the GNE method is that it measures unemployment in terms of the units (dollars of 1935–9 purchasing power) in which other magnitudes are measured. Although in one sense this is a minor point and involves matters of statistical convenience rather than of economic substance, it also avoids an additional source of error. When the GNE measure of unemployment is used, the effect of any change in economic conditions on the amount of unemployment so measured is known as soon as the effect on the GNE (at 1935–9 prices) is known. If we were to begin by using the number of unemployed as our measure, an additional source of error would be introduced, since the relationship between numbers employed and GNE, although it would be expected to be a very close one, is of a stochastic nature.

The measure of unemployment described above has distinct advantages for this study in that it is theoretically more defensible and statistically both more accurate and more convenient to use than is the alternative method,[3] but in practice the differences between the two measures are likely to be much less important. In theory, the unemployment of all the factors of production should be considered, but in practice, the extent to which there is unemployment of labour is almost certain to be a reasonably accurate index of all unemployment. In the first place, the return to labour amounts to not less than 70 per cent of the total payment to all factors; measured by the return it receives, labour is approximately twice as important as all other factors combined.[4] In the second place, because of the importance of labour, the cyclical variations in the employment of other factors tend to be closely correlated with variations in the employment of labour.[5] For these reasons, if the amount of unemployment of labour can be determined it will almost certainly give a reasonably accurate indication of the unemployment of all factors.

Again, it is quite true that all labour is not equally productive, but this assumption is not likely to introduce serious error. Examination of the statistical evidence in Table VIII, suggests that variations in average labour productivity are influenced more by other secular and cyclical factors than by short-term differences in the average quality of the labour employed. One might expect that the more efficient labour would tend to be continued in employment in periods of decline, and that in periods of expansion the less efficient labour would be gradually taken back into employment. However, the figures in Table VIII show that average productivity has just the opposite cyclical pattern to that implied by this argument, and we conclude that any such cyclical fluctuations as there may have been in the average quality of the labour force are more than offset by other influences. Thus, although it is essential to be aware of the theoretical issues involved in choosing between these two measures of unemployment, it is also important not to discard on purely *a priori* grounds a measure which may, in practice, be found very useful.

Since it appears, therefore, that the amount of unemployment can best be measured in terms of the shortfall of actual GNE below the full employment GNE (both at 1935-9 prices), the next step must be to establish the precise meaning of full employment. There may be said to be no cyclical unemployment in an economy when an increase in aggregate effective demand would lead to a rise in prices rather than to an increase in output.[6] For, if there is full employment of the factors of production, it will not be possible (in the absence of technological advance) to increase output in the aggregate. Consequently, an increase in aggregate demand will be reflected in rising prices rather than in increased production.

This statement establishes the principle, but it cannot be applied with great precision to determine whether or not there was full employment in any specific case. An economy is not a monolithic structure, but rather an agglomeration of heterogeneous elements. Thus some sectors may be experiencing overfull employment at a time when there are unemployed resources in others. The market may be temporarily oversupplied with some items, individuals may be temporarily unemployed as they change jobs, seasonal factors may cause temporary reduction or cessation of production in some industries, and so on. The limits of the productive capacity of the economy in the aggregate will be reached while there is some unemployment in particular industries or localities.

In addition, a certain vagueness is inseparable from the concept of full employment, since the term would appear to mean the employment of the total supply (subject to the qualifications noted in the preceding paragraph) of the factors of production. But what factors are to be included? Before the economy in general reaches full employment there will be shortages in some sectors. These shortages will cause the prices of the products concerned to rise relative to the general level of prices and so make it profitable, if it is technologically possible, to employ factors of production which would normally be submarginal. At the same time, in other industries which have not yet reached full employment, there will be unemployed factors which are intramarginal in the sense that they are not less efficient than factors that are already employed.

It is apparent that a state of absolute full employment is never likely to be attained. A national economy contains many factors of production and at any given time some of them will inevitably be unemployed. Moreover, an increase in aggregate demand will in most cases lead *both* to some increase in output *and* to some increase in prices. Thus it will be found that prices begin to rise before a state which could be considered one of full employment is reached and that there will continue to be an increase in output up to a point beyond that at which full employment (on any reasonable appraisal) is attained. Although no estimate of a full employment income for any year can be made with great precision, it is convenient for some purposes to have a single figure which is felt to be the best approximation to what a full employment income would have been for that year; but it should be clear that any such figure can be only an approximation, and that it is subject to some not insignificant margin of indeterminacy. A more valid procedure is to attempt to designate the range within which the most probable full employment income figure seems likely to be found and to recognize that any single figure can be no more than an approximation.

The discussion of the theoretical issues has now been completed and it is time to consider how best to attack the specific problem which confronts us here, i.e., how to estimate the amount by which the actual GNE at 1935–9 prices in each of the years with which we are concerned fell short of what a full employment income would have been.

The first step is to look for the years in which full employment seems, *prima facie*, to have been realized or most closely approached. The years 1929 and 1941 were found to be most satisfactory for this purpose. For these two years estimates of what a full employment income would have been were made. The estimates for the other years were derived from the figures for these two bench-mark years. A more detailed account of the method of deriving these figures is given in Appendix C.

The estimates exclude the agricultural sector of the economy. In this industry we find that large variations in production are the result primarily of varying weather conditions during the crop-growing period. By excluding agriculture we exclude most of the effects of these random disturbances, which are irrelevant for our purposes.[7]

It has been mentioned above that no single figure for a full employment income can be regarded as more than an approximation. It was, therefore, necessary to fix, in addition to the single figure which seemed most appropriate, the upper and lower limits of the range which we could be reasonably confident would contain the desired figure. These upper and lower limits were estimated for 1929 and 1941 and, from the figures for these two years, the corresponding figures appropriate to the other years of the period were derived.

The final results of these calculations are shown in Table VIII. In this table only that figure which is considered the best estimate for each year is shown. The range in the estimates of full employment GNE is of the order of 4 per cent either way from this figure to the values shown for the upper and lower limits. All three figures for each year will be found in Appendix C, Table XXIV, and are shown graphically below Table VIII.

The statistics in Table VIII show that the realized GNE did not fall far short of the full employment level in any of the years 1926–9. There was a substantial increase in the amount of unemployment in 1930 and a sharp further increase in 1931; thereafter, the figure for the deficiency of GNE below full employment was never less than $1·5 billion in any year until 1941. The maximum figure, slightly more than $2¼ billion, was reached in 1933.

B

TABLE VIII
THE AMOUNT OF UNEMPLOYMENT IN CANADA 1926–41 (all dollar figures at 1935–9 prices)

Year	Full employment GNE (millions)	Realized GNE (millions)	Deficiency of realized GNE relative to full employment GNE (millions)	Deficiency as % of full employment GNE	Number unemployed as % of non-agr. labour force*	Non-agr. GNE Per Capita
1926	$4,046	$3,927	$ 119	2·9	2·5	$1,750
1927	4,386	4,335	51	1·2	1·0	1,842
1928	4,778	4,748	30	0·6	1·0	1,939
1929	5,117	4,965	152	3·0	2·5	2,002
1930	5,353	4,773	580	10·8	12·0	1,997
1931	5,574	4,162	1,412	25·3	16·0	1,782
1932	5,743	3,869	1,874	32·6	25·0	1,760
1933	5,918	3,650	2,268	38·3	27·0	1,718
1934	6,114	3,997	2,117	34·6	21·0	1,652
1935	6,274	4,267	2,007	32·0	19·0	1,687
1936	6,461	4,489	1,972	30·5	17·0	1,709
1937	6,636	4,886	1,750	26·4	12·0	1,759
1938	6,825	4,842	1,983	29·1	16·0	1,786
1939	7,050	5,191	1,859	26·4	†	1,874
1940	7,305	5,763	1,542	21·1	†	1,969
1941	7,390	6,553	837	13·3	†	2,152

*The percentage unemployed as calculated from the official figures was adjusted from a June 1 to an annual basis and then reduced by 3·5 percentage points to permit comparison with the figures in the preceding column.
†Not calculated for the war years.

Sources: Tables xxii, xxiv and *National Accounts*, Appendix, Table ii.

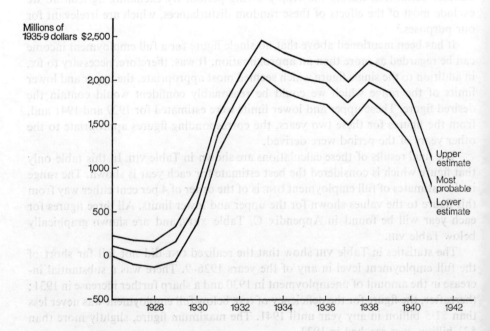

From these absolute figures, together with our estimate of what a full employment at GNE would have been, it is possible to calculate a relative measure of unemployment for each year, i.e., the percentage by which the realized GNE in each year was less than the estimated full employment income for that year. On this basis we find that the percentage unemployment was relatively low (never in excess of 3 per cent) in the years 1926-9. It increased to over 10 per cent in 1930 and thereafter never fell below 25 per cent in any year until 1940. In the worst year of the depression, 1933, the actual GNE was 38 per cent below the estimated full employment GNE for that year. This figure is derived from the "most probable" estimate; even if we use the lower estimate the figure is 36 per cent.

Table VIII also shows the percentage of individuals in the non-agricultural labour force who were unemployed as calculated from the official statistics, adjusted as explained in the footnote to permit comparison with the GNE measure of unemployment. In the prosperous early part of the period (1926-9), the two measures of unemployment differ only slightly (although this is due in part to the method of estimating the full employment GNE in those years). By 1931 the GNE measure of unemployment is more than one and one-half times as great as the labour force unemployment estimate for the non-agricultural sectors. Except in 1932 and 1933, the GNE figure remained more than one-half greater than the alternative measure until after 1938.[8]

A brief digression seems in order here to consider some of the possible reasons for the substantial differences, especially during depression, between these measures of unemployment. Two reasons were mentioned in the general discussion at the beginning of this chapter, the prevalence of short time and of disguised unemployment (especially in agriculture and among the self-employed); this latter factor is likely to become increasingly important during a prolonged depression such as that of the 1930s. The labour force figures, which show larger numbers in agriculture and among the self-employed in the middle 1930s than in more prosperous years, indicate that this factor was operative in our period. It is also true that a higher proportion of employed workers were working only part-time in the depression years, but, unfortunately, we have no adequate data on which to base an estimate of the quantitative importance of this factor.

A third factor, which has not been mentioned previously in this study, seems likely to have been present. This is the probable reduction in average productivity of the labour force when production levels fall substantially below the full employment position. During periods of prosperity, such as the late 1920s, productive facilities are developed which are designed for these conditions. Then, when demand falls off as it did during the 1930s, the firms are left with the fixed or overhead expense appropriate to higher levels of output. The number of executive, supervisory, and maintenance employees cannot be reduced in proportion to the fall in output, so that, in effect, there is a form of underemployment of these workers. In addition, those who are engaged directly in production may not be as effectively employed when plants are working well below the outputs for which they were designed. Thus output is likely to fall more than in proportion to the decline in the number of people employed, i.e., there is a fall in per capita productivity.

The figures in the last column of Table VIII do show a sharp decline on the average in the annual output of employed non-agricultural workers after 1930. In fact, if we assume that productivity would have increased after 1929 at a compound rate of 2 per cent a year[9] under full employment, then the actual non-agricultural GNE per capita in 1934 (when it reached its lowest figure) was only 75 per cent of what it would have been. In part this reduced average output is explained by the two factors of disguised unemployment and short-time work for some of those who were still employed, but it seems probable that this third factor was also of more than negligible importance.[10] And, of course, each of these three factors would contribute to making the GNE measure of unemployment greater than would appear from a measure of the number of individuals who were unemployed.

Finally, there is another factor which suggests that even the GNE measure of unemployment is, from one point of view at least, biased downwards. Under conditions of continuing prosperity we could reasonably expect the GNE per capita to increase at a rate of somewhere in the neighbourhood of 2 per cent per year. During depression, however, the cyclical decline in productivity also has an effect on longer-term growth. Thus, although 1941 was a more prosperous year than was 1930, and so cyclical factors would be favourable to higher productivity in that year, we find that the average annual rate of increase in non-agricultural GNE over the period 1930–41 was only about 0·8 per cent per annum. If we had assumed a 2 per cent annual increase in output per capita, the full employment GNE would have been higher and the GNE measure of unemployment likewise would have been a larger figure than the one we have used.

Nor does this exhaust the effects of depression on the level of income. The fact that productivity increases more slowly during depression implies that after the return of prosperity the full employment income will be lower than it would have been if there had been no depression. The low rate of growth of the capital stock during depression provides a part of the explanation for this. In addition, individuals who suffer prolonged unemployment or whose special skills remain unused for long periods will be less productive when they are brought back to work than if they had been using their skills continuously. Consequently, although the measure of unemployment we have used seems more adequate for our purposes than would be the measure based on the number of unemployed individuals it, too, seems to understate the real cost of long-continued depression. Our estimates do, however, give a satisfactory general indication of the contours of prosperity and depression in the period 1926–41, and that is sufficient for our purposes.

4
Canada's Current
Account Credits

In this chapter we shall consider the factors which seem to have been important in influencing the level of Canada's current account credits and shall test their importance empirically. In particular, we want to test the hypothesis which was developed in Chapter 1. The essence of this theory was that, as incomes in other countries varied, spending in these countries on goods and services provided by Canada would vary in the same direction and according to some stable, but presumably stochastic, relationship. This simple, basic hypothesis requires modification to allow for the possibility that there may have been changes in the prices of Canada's exports relative to world price levels, changes in the ratio of domestic costs in Canada to export prices, changes in the commercial policies of other countries (especially those which are major purchasers of Canadian exports), and a variety of other possible changes which are discussed more fully later in this chapter.

We shall begin our investigation by setting out the regression model which will be used. We shall then consider, and attempt to assess in general terms, the importance of various possible disturbing factors which are not taken into account explicitly in the model. Next, the results of the regression analysis will be presented, evaluated, and the original approach will be modified if the evidence suggests that changes would be desirable. Finally, we shall summarize the conclusions, indicating in what respects the original hypothesis is confirmed and what modifications or changes in emphasis seem to be appropriate.

Exports of "grains and farinaceous products" have been excluded from the figures used in this chapter for reasons which are developed in some detail in Appendix D. The value of non-monetary gold exports is included, but Appendix E gives the regression equation when this item is excluded. Appendix F is devoted to an analysis of Canada's current account credits with the United States. This separate treatment of Canada's largest export market provides both a measure of disaggregation and an additional test of the hypothesis.[1]

The problem before us may be viewed largely, although not entirely, as one of developing and testing a demand function for Canada's exports of goods and services.[2] It is convenient to view the matter in this fashion, since by so doing we are able to draw on the substantial body of doctrine which has been developed in relation to the theory of demand and the derivation of demand functions. The function which is relevant here is, however, one of unusual complexity for reasons explained below.

The general regression equation which is employed in this chapter is of the form

$$X = a + b_1 Y + b_2 P + b_3 C + u,$$

where the symbols used have the following meanings:

X is Canada's exports of goods and services (including non-monetary gold but excluding grains and farinaceous products) valued at 1935–9 prices and adjusted for changes in population in the purchasing countries.

a is the constant term in the regression equation.

Y is the index of real income, adjusted for population changes, in the purchasing countries.

P is the ratio of the price of Canada's exports of goods and services to the relevant domestic prices in the importing countries. A special adjustment factor to allow for changes in commercial policy in the importing countries is incorporated in this variable.

C is the ratio of the price index for Canada's exports of goods and services to an index of domestic costs of production.

u is the residual error term. The residuals are assumed to be normally distributed with a mean of 0.

b_1, b_2, and b_3 are the regression coefficients which relate changes in Y, P, and C, respectively, to the associated changes in X.

The derivation of the statistical series for the four variables (X, Y, P, and C) is explained in Appendix H. The series themselves are brought together in Table IX.

TABLE IX
SUMMARY OF ORIGINAL TIME SERIES AND FIRST DIFFERENCES REQUIRED
FOR REGRESSION ANALYSIS FOR EXPORTS

	Original time series data				First differences			
Year	Exports* (X)	Income in other countries (Y)	Relative prices (P)	Supply factor (C)	X	Y	P	C
1926	$ 935	93·7	105·0	130·9				
1927	940	95·4	105·9	124·9	+ 5	+1·7	+0·9	− 6·0
1928	981	96·0	104·5	121·6	+ 41	+0·6	−1·4	− 3·3
1929	1,047	99·6	105·6	119·1	+ 66	+3·6	+1·1	− 2·5
1930	899	92·0	106·1	104·3	−148	−7·6	+0·5	−14·8
1931	779	85·3	110·0	95·5	−120	−6·7	+3·9	− 8·8
1932	679	76·4	111·0	93·8	−100	−8·9	+1·0	− 1·7
1933	712	77·9	105·7	98·6	+ 33	+1·5	−5·3	+ 4·8
1934	843	84·1	101·6	103·1	+131	+6·2	−4·1	+ 4·5
1935	933	90·5	98·0	101·3	+ 90	+6·4	−3·6	− 1·8
1936	1,084	100·0	98·6	103·2	+151	+9·5	+0·6	+ 1·9
1937	1,230	103·9	97·8	103·6	+146	+3·9	−0·8	+ 0·4
1938	1,086	100·2	102·6	97·1	−144	−3·7	+4·8	− 6·5

*This series is in millions of dollars at 1935–9 prices and adjusted for population (1926=100).

It will be convenient throughout the remainder of this chapter to use the term *exports* to mean the value of the variable X calculated in the manner described above.

We have specified the variables that will be used in the regression analysis, and the reasons for using the first differences rather than the original data are given in Appendix A (on econometric methods). The factors which have not been taken into account in some way in the calculations are assumed to have remained unchanged or to have been of such slight importance as not to have influenced the volume of Canada's exports to any major extent.

In order to review the assumptions it is convenient to consider them in four groups, which correspond to four features of the export function as set out above. For the first two, we examine the assumptions which are relevant, respectively, to micro-economic and to macro-economic demand functions. Third, we must consider the special complications that arise because we are dealing with trade between nations. Finally, we consider the possibility that disturbing factors arise in relation to the supply factor.

A simple, micro-economic demand function shows the relationship between the price of a good and the quantity traded in the market, assuming that there are no changes in incomes, other prices, population, tastes, or expectations. Income appears as a separate variable in our equation. By using a price ratio rather than absolute prices, we have attempted to make provision for the effects of changes in other prices. All incomes and quantities traded have been adjusted for population change.

We have still to consider the possible influence of changes in tastes and in expectations. Here the "tastes" with which we are concerned are not merely the state of consumer preferences with respect to one good or service, but rather the attitudes and requirements of consumers, industrial users, and borrowers in many other countries with respect to purchases of the considerable range of Canadian goods and services which are offered for sale in the export market. For example, the "tastes" which are relevant in this context would include the preference (or otherwise) of the consumer in the United Kingdom for Canadian bacon, the technological "preference" of United States newspaper presses for Canadian newsprint, and the preference of borrowers in other countries for continuing to borrow from Canada and to pay the return on their borrowings.

Sudden changes in "tastes" which would have a large effect on the aggregate of Canada's exports are likely to occur very rarely; there seem to have been no striking cases of such changes from 1926 to 1938. The more gradual changes which are taking place all the time are taken into account through the trend term in the regression equation.[3]

Changes in expectations may also affect demand substantially over fairly short periods of a few days or weeks. But we deal with annual data and, in general, one would not expect changes in expectations to have much effect on the annual figures or, more relevantly here, on the year-to-year changes. The most important exception which seems at all probable, and which is relevant to this study, arises in connection with changes in commercial policy, and even here there are other opposing influences which would tend to dampen this force.

There are three general points here which suggest that the effect of tariff changes on behaviour as a result of changes in expectations is unlikely to be great. First, our analysis is based on annual data and expectations are likely to operate for somewhat shorter periods than a year for the type of transaction involved here. Second, there are costs (such as financing and storage) involved in building up stocks to anticipate tariff increases and there are the inconveniences and possible loss of business which result from buying less and reducing stocks in anticipation of tariff reductions. Third, tariffs are likely to be increased when prices and sales are falling. At such times businessmen will be reluctant to increase stocks greatly even to anticipate a tariff increase. Conversely, tariffs are likely to be reduced, if at all, when prices and sales are rising, and in these circumstances there will be reluctance to reduce stocks in anticipation of tariff reductions. For all these reasons it seems unlikely that changes in expectations had much effect on the data we are examining.

When we consider the properties of the export function which are similar to those of an aggregate demand function, the principal assumption we have to examine involves the distribution of expenditure. We would expect that within a given country the distribution of expenditure among the various types of goods and services would be closely correlated with the level of income, and income is a variable in the regression equation. There was a good deal of similarity in the behaviour of income for the different countries (as shown in Appendix H, Table XLII), but it will be noted that income in the United Kingdom rose less in the early years, fell less in the depression, and recovered more quickly and more completely than did income in the United States. If the income elasticity of demand for Canada's exports were substantially different in these two countries, there could be some effect on Canada's exports from this source. The separate treatment in Appendix F of exports to the United States is relevant in this context.

The fact that we are dealing with trade between nations means that we must consider fluctuations in exchange rates and in commercial policy. Exports and incomes have been expressed in real terms, which are, at least in principle, independent of exchange rates. All prices have been converted from the original currency to the Canadian dollar equivalent.

Commercial policy cannot be dismissed so lightly. After 1929, nations used commercial policy in many forms (of which tariffs were only one important class) to check the flow of imports, and there can be no doubt that these measures had substantial effect. The price equivalent of the tariff, which we have used to measure commercial policy, is biased downward for reasons which are discussed in Appendix H. However, examination of the price series used shows that relative prices (including the price equivalent of the tariffs imposed on them) of Canadian exports had an upward trend when the influence of protectionist commercial policy was increasing most rapidly and that they had a downward trend when there was the most marked reversal of this protectionist tendency between 1934 and 1936.[4] The more exact representation of commercial policy in the prices used would have accentuated these trends, but would not have changed their general direction. Although this fact may give some reassurance, it remains true that the possible errors in measurement in relation to commercial policy are probably the most serious source of distortion considered. This is inconvenient for this study, but is not surprising since commercial policy is expressly designed to affect the commodity composition as well as the magnitude of international trade.

Our treatment of the export function up to this point has been focused on demand influences and we must now consider how supply factors may be taken into account. Let us suppose that, associated with a given level of exports from Canada, there is a given level of income in the rest of the world, of relative prices for Canadian exports compared with world prices, a given structure of commercial policies, and a given level of costs of production in Canada. We now assume that there is a sharp increase in these costs of production, all the other determinants of exports we are considering remaining unchanged.[5] There has been no new factor operating directly to change either of the first two explanatory variables which we have in our equation (world income and relative prices), and yet it is clear that this rise in domestic cost levels in Canada will cause a reduction in exports except in the improbable case where their supply is perfectly inelastic with respect to cost changes in the relevant range. How should we deal with this change in conditions of supply?

When it is necessary to consider both demand and supply factors in an economic relationship, the standard econometric procedure is to employ the simultaneous equations technique, convert these equations to their reduced forms, and solve to derive the estimated values of the required coefficients. In the present instance, however, we have only one endogenous variable, the quantity of exports. Since price can be taken as being determined by world market conditions (on which, in the aggregate, Canada has only a minor effect), it is appropriate to treat it as an exogenous factor in our model. What is required is a single equation which will give the relationship between the exogenous explanatory variables on the one hand and the single endogenous variable, quantity of exports, on the other.

In this case, therefore, the appropriate procedure in deriving the export equation is to compute the regression of the dependent variable, X, on the three independent variables, Y, P, and C, as these have been defined above. The detailed explanation of the derivation of the four time series is given in Appendix H, so we can proceed directly here to a consideration of the results of the regression analysis.

The multiple regression equation[6] calculated from the first differences of the four time series is:

$$X = \$15 \cdot 0 \text{ million} + 14 \cdot 18Y - 3 \cdot 88P + 3 \cdot 86C.$$
$$(2 \cdot 91) \quad (5 \cdot 24) \quad (3 \cdot 27)$$

The standard error of estimate for this equation is $32·6 million. The coefficient of multiple determination (R^2) is $0·910$ and it is significant at the $0·001$ level. The corrected coefficient of multiple correlation ($\bar{R}$) is $0·936$. The von Neumann ratio is $3·00$, which does not suggest the presence of serial correlation in the residuals.[7] The number in parentheses under each regression coefficient is the standard error of that coefficient.[8]

These results are, in most respects, satisfactory. The corrected coefficient of multiple correlation is much higher than would be required for significance at the conventional $0·05$ level. The regression coefficients all have the signs which economic theory would lead us to expect. The equation as a whole accounts for slightly more than 90 per cent of the fluctuations in exports (i.e., $R^2 = 0·910$), leaving less than 10 per cent dependent upon factors not represented in the equation or upon stochastic disturbances. The regression coefficient for the income term is almost five times its own standard error and is therefore significantly different from zero. In all

B*

these respects the results are acceptable in terms of both the economic and the statistical criteria.

With respect to the regression coefficients of the other two explanatory variables and the pattern shown by the individual year-by-year residuals, matters are less satisfactory. The regression coefficient for the price term (P) contains its standard error only 0·74 times and so it is not significantly different from zero at any reasonable confidence level. Two reasons may be advanced for the poor showing of the price coefficient here. First, there is the difficulty, which we have discussed above, of measuring the price equivalent of changes in commercial policy. Second, there is the fact that the price variable did not fluctuate widely in this period. (This is understandable since it measures changes in *relative* prices and not changes in the absolute level of the price index for exports.) For example, the standard deviation of the first differences of the relative price series is only 2·9 compared with a standard deviation of 5·7 for the income variable and 5·4 for the cost variable. This means, in a stochastic relationship such as we have here, that the effects of the fluctuations in the other variables with their larger regression coefficients could obscure the influence of the changes in the price variable. If, in fact, the true value of the price coefficient is, in absolute terms, no larger than of the order of 2 or 3, and the other circumstances of the period are as our time series indicate, we simply have not the data to permit us to make a more precise estimate of the coefficient of the price variable.

For the supply coefficient the same considerations apply, but with diminished force. This variable contains its standard error 1·18 times, so there is about one chance in seven that its true value is not greater than zero. The results for this variable are thus distinctly better than for the price variable.

In all the calculations in this study the data have been adjusted to take account of changes in population. In terms of economic theory this seems desirable because it permits a distinction between, for example, the effects of an increase in national income which results from an increase in population and one which comes about because of an increase in per capita productivity. Since there is no *a priori* reason to expect the results of a change in income to be the same in the two cases, it is desirable, if we are thinking in terms of the economic theory involved, to use a method which differentiates between them. But, on statistical grounds, there is the consideration that if, to use the example of this chapter, we adjust both exports and income in this way, the effect will be to increase the coefficient of correlation compared with what it would have been if the data had not been adjusted for population change. In order to test the importance of this factor a regression equation was computed from the data used above except that the export and income series were not adjusted for population change.

The regression equation for the period 1927–38 is:

$$X = \$11 \cdot 0 \text{ million} + 15 \cdot 14Y - 5 \cdot 65P + 4 \cdot 48C.$$
$$(3 \cdot 47) \quad (6 \cdot 38) \quad (4 \cdot 02)$$

$R^2 = 0 \cdot 882$ and $\bar{R} = 0 \cdot 915$ so that the coefficient of multiple correlation is significant at the 0·001 level. The standard error of estimate is \$40.0 million and the von Neumann ratio is 2·48.

An appraisal of these results would yield conclusions which would not differ in any important respect from those obtained in the preceding regression. In these circumstances it seems desirable, for the reason given above, to use the data which have been adjusted for population change.

The residuals from the regression equation using such data were calculated for each year, and are shown in Table x, along with the actual and the calculated year-to-year changes in the export variable.

TABLE X

COMPARISON OF ACTUAL AND COMPUTED
VALUES FOR THE EXPORT VARIABLE

Year	Actual value X_a	Computed value* X_c	Residuals† $(X_a - X_c)$	
			D_1	D_2
1927	+ 5	+ 13	− 8	−12
1928	+ 41	+ 16	+25	+30
1929	+ 66	+ 52	+14	+ 8
1930	−148	−152	+ 4	0
1931	−120	−129	+ 9	−13
1932	−100	−122	+22	+ 8
1933	+ 33	+ 75	−42	−23
1934	+131	+136	− 5	+12
1935	+ 90	+113	−23	− 5
1936	+151	+155	− 4	− 5
1937	+146	+ 75	+71	
1938	−144	− 81	−63	

*Derived from the first regression equation which is based on the entire period 1927–38.
†The D_1 residuals are computed from the first two columns of the table. The D_2 values are the residuals calculated from the second regression equation (from which 1937 and 1938 have been omitted).

The first thing noticed from the first two columns of Table x, is that the computed values not only move generally in close conformity with the actual values (as we know they must do for the coefficient of correlation to be as high as it is), but that in every year of the period the computed value changed in the same direction as the actual value; in every year we would get a better estimate of the export variable from our equation than would be obtained from just assuming that it would be unchanged from the preceding year.

The residuals were calculated for each year and are shown in the third column of the table. Examination of these residuals reveals a pronounced tendency for positive signs to predominate in years of contraction and for negative signs to appear in years of expansion. The exceptions to this general rule occur only in 1928 and 1929 and in 1937 and 1938. This immediately suggests a lag of the export variable, and this would also be plausible, although not essential, in terms of the economic causation postulated in this study.[9]

A lagged regression was calculated, but it did not bring the expected improvement in the time pattern of the residuals; the pattern was, if anything, less satisfactory than before, and so it was necessary to consider other possible causes of this difficulty with the residuals. Further examination of the actual and computed values from the first regression shows that, for the years 1927–36, the year-to-year figures for the computed values of the export variable, i.e., changes in the value of exports, were greater than the actual values except for the years 1928 and 1929. In 1937 and 1938 this pattern was reversed; the computed values were large but just slightly more than half as large as the actual changes in each of these two years.

The explanation of these events appears to lie in the rather unusual economic circumstances which prevailed in world trade in 1937 and 1938. In 1937 Canada's exports increased much more than the regression equation would lead us to expect and in 1938 they fell by much more than would be expected. For the world as a whole, incomes and prices rose rapidly in the last quarter of 1936 and in the early months of 1937. This rapid expansion was followed, in the last quarter of 1937 and throughout most of 1938, by a sharp contraction.[10]

The response of importers was to buy in excess of their current requirements during most of 1937. Then, in 1938, after the sharp downturn toward the end of 1937, they bought less than required to provide for current production and sales as they reduced their excess inventories accumulated in the previous year.

In summary, world trade seems to have experienced the effects of destabilizing speculative buying in 1937 and the converse of this in 1938. The assumption we have made that there were no changes in expectations would appear to be invalid for these two years.

The effect of including 1937 and 1938, when the influence of expectations was great, is to distort the regression for the period as a whole because, through the effect of the squaring process, the large values in these two years are given considerable weight in relation to the period as a whole.[11] As a result, the equation for the entire period is distorted, and distorted in precisely that way which would produce the pattern of residuals we have observed, i.e., the calculated values for the changes in exports up to the end of 1936 were generally larger (ignoring the sign) than were the actual changes.

This finding suggests that we should expect to obtain more satisfactory results in the pattern of the residuals by computing a regression similar to that above but with the years 1937 and 1938 omitted. The regression equation which results is:

$$X = \$18 \cdot 9 \text{ million} + 13 \cdot 56Y + 0 \cdot 84P + 4 \cdot 33C.$$
$$\phantom{X = \$18 \cdot 9 \text{ million} + } (1 \cdot 27) \quad (2 \cdot 84) \quad (1 \cdot 56)$$

The standard error of estimate is $\$14 \cdot 2$ million. $R^2 = 0 \cdot 980$ and $\bar{R} = 0 \cdot 985$, which is significant at the $0 \cdot 001$ level. The von Neumann ratio is $2 \cdot 91$, which does not suggest either positive or negative serial correlation in the residuals.[12]

Evaluation of this equation shows that it is an improvement over its predecessors. The coefficient of correlation, which was significant at the $0 \cdot 001$ level before, has increased further and, more conspicuously, the standard error of estimate is less than half what it was for the first regression. The constant term is still positive and is somewhat larger than before. The coefficient of the income variable is slightly smaller, but now contains its own standard error more than ten times rather than about five times as in the earlier calculations. The price coefficient is positive but is less than its own standard error and so is not significantly different from zero. The coefficient of the supply factor is slightly larger than in the first equation and is now 2·78 times its own standard error. It is significant here at the 0·025 level, where before it was not significant at the 0·10 level.

The behaviour of the residuals is also much better in this equation. As implied by the smaller standard error of estimate, the residuals are smaller than in the previous case, most conspicuously in years when the residuals were largest for the earlier equation. The pattern of the signs of the residuals has also improved; by a crude test, there are six changes of sign for the residuals in this case compared with only two for the same period in the first equation.

We are now in a position to bring together the conclusions suggested by the analysis in this chapter and to comment on the original hypothesis in the light of these conclusions. The summary below considers the two regressions, the original one for the entire period (which we shall designate regression I) and the regression omitting the years 1937 and 1938 (which we shall designate regression II).

The conclusions may be presented in the following six points:

1   Canada's exports of grains and farinaceous products depend upon the supply available from the carryover plus the current crop. Income in other countries was found to be unimportant in determining the volume of exports in this group. These items were excluded from all the subsequent regression analyses. The evidence in support of this conclusion will be found in Appendix D.

2   Both regression I and regression II gave good results, but the latter is a considerable improvement over the former. In both cases the coefficient of multiple correlation is significant at the 0·001 level. In neither case does the value of the von Neumann ratio suggest the presence of serial correlation in the residuals. The first equation explains 91 per cent of the variance in the export variable, and the second 98 per cent.

3   Income fluctuations emerge clearly as the dominant factor influencing the fluctuations in exports. In both regressions, the coefficient of the income variable was significant at the 0·001 level. It was also highly stable, with values of 14·18 and 13·56 respectively.

4   The price variable was not found to be statistically significant in either case. It has already been suggested that the small fluctuations in this variable, the difficulties with the price equivalent of commercial policy, and the dominant role of the income variable have combined to obscure the influence that may have been exerted by changes in relative prices.

5   The supply factor emerges as one whose influence should not be overlooked. It is statistically significant at the 0·025 level in regression II (but not in regression I). It is also reasonably stable, with values of 3·86 and 4·33. It accounts for 15 per cent of the variance in exports in the first regression and for 19 per cent in the second.

6   Changes in expectations in 1937–8 appear to have had a considerable influence on the equation for the entire period. Because of this factor, the equation for the period which omits 1937 and 1938 is preferred to the equation for the entire period.

We conclude that our hypothesis concerning the importance of incomes in the rest of the world for the volume of exports of goods and services from Canada has been sustained except for the special case of grains and farinaceous products. The income hypothesis is applicable to other exports, but it needs to be broadened to include consideration of the supply factor and to recognize that the influence of changes in expectations in particular years can have a major effect. The original hypothesis, amended in these respects, gives a good explanation of the behaviour of Canada's exports in the 1926–38 period.

5

Canada's Demand for Imports

This is the second of three chapters which are concerned with deriving some of the basic relationships for the Canadian economy in the period 1926–38. In Chapter 4 we have considered, and endeavoured to develop an explanation for, the fluctuations in Canada's export of goods and services. In Chapter 6 we examine the influences which seem to have played the dominant roles in bringing about fluctuations in the GNE. This chapter is concerned with developing and testing statistically an explanation of the behaviour of imports of goods and services into Canada in the period 1926–38.

An understanding of this relationship is important for an understanding of the general functioning of the Canadian economy, and it is also important for purposes of national economic policy. This is especially true if we are considering a policy designed to increase incomes in a period of depression because the increase in imports which is likely to accompany the desired increase in incomes may present a major obstacle to the success of such an expansionist policy. The general question of the implications of this study for economic policy will be considered in Chapter 8. Our primary concern here is not, however, with economic policy, but with developing and testing an explanation of the behaviour of imports.

Our treatment of this question is developed in four stages. First, we set out the import function in the form to be used and describe the content of each variable in it. Second, we consider what seem likely, on *a priori* grounds, to be the major sources of disturbance to the relationship postulated. Third, we compute the values of the parameters in the regression equation and evaluate these for statistical significance and economic plausibility. Finally, the results obtained in Appendix G from disaggregating imports into twelve groups are compared with those obtained when the single equation for all imports is used.

We can state that, *ceteris paribus*, imports of goods and services will be expected to vary directly with income in the importing country and inversely with the prices of such imports compared with the relevant domestic prices in the importing country. The general form of the import equation expressing this relationship is:

$$M = a + b_1 Y + b_2 (P_{MT}/P_D) + u,$$

where:
M is imports of goods and services.
a is the constant term in the equation.

b_1 is the coefficient which relates changes in income to changes in imports or, more technically, the marginal propensity to import.

Y is the relevant measure of national income.

b_2 is the coefficient which relates changes in the relative prices of imports to changes in the imports. If income is kept constant, b_2 is the slope of the demand curve for imports.

P_{MT} is the price index (including adjustment for tariffs) for imports of goods and services.

P_D is the domestic price index which is relevant to the demand for imports.

u is the residual error term, assumed to be normally distributed with a mean of zero.

The regression equation was calculated from the first differences rather than from the original data for reasons which are discussed in Appendix A. The sources and methods used to derive the time series are considered in Appendix I. The results of the calculations, i.e., the data used in the regression analysis, are shown in Table XI.

TABLE XI
ORIGINAL TIME SERIES AND FIRST DIFFERENCES FOR AGGREGATE
REGRESSION – IMPORTS

	Original time series			First differences		
Year	Imports per capita	Income per capita	Relative prices	Import variable	Income variable	Price variable
1926	$123·2	$472	110			
1927	135·7	502	109	$+ 12·5	$+ 30	−1
1928	150·6	541	110	+ 14·9	+ 39	+1
1929	160·7	538	108	+ 10·1	− 3	−2
1930	146·2	489	103	− 14·5	− 49	−5
1931	112·7	428	106	− 33·5	− 61	+3
1932	90·1	367	110	− 22·6	− 61	+4
1933	85·5	351	106	− 4·6	− 16	−4
1934	90·9	387	104	+ 5·4	+ 36	−2
1935	98·4	413	101	+ 7·5	+ 26	−3
1936	110·8	433	100	+ 12·4	+ 20	−1
1937	119·2	470	100	+ 8·4	+ 37	0
1938	113·2	463	99	− 6·0	− 7	−1

The function which concerns us here for Canada's imports is, in most aspects, analogous to the one considered in the preceding chapter for Canada's exports.[1] Consequently, it is not necessary to repeat the review of assumptions included there and we can proceed directly to a consideration of what seem most likely, on *a priori* grounds, to be the major possible sources of disturbance to the relationship to be computed. Three such sources of disturbance will be mentioned.

The first arises because of changes in the distribution of expenditure among the various spending sectors. This can have a disturbing influence because some components of expenditure have a higher import content than have others, and there may be substantial variation from sector to sector in this respect.[2] It is possible that disturbances arising from changes in the distribution of outlay may be of more than negligible magnitude.[3]

Secondly, we have changes in the administrative aspects of commercial policy.

These have not been taken into account explicitly in our equation because they cannot be reduced to precise quantitative terms, but it seems highly probable that the height of administrative barriers to imports will be positively correlated with changes in tariff rates and negatively correlated, in the short run, with changes in the level of domestic expenditure. Consequently, the effects of such administrative changes will be reflected, at least in a broad way, in other variables which are directly represented in the import equation. In view of the difficulty of applying a numerical assessment to this factor directly, we may conclude that the method used is reasonably satisfactory and that we would expect (we cannot be dogmatic about this) only relatively minor disturbances to the computed relationship from this source.

Thirdly, we consider changes in expectations. Since we are using annual data we would not expect these changes to be of any major significance. However, in view of our findings in Chapter 4, we might be more inclined to look for evidence of destabilizing speculation in 1937 and 1938. But Canada's exports consist largely of raw materials and partially manufactured products, for which prices tend to fluctuate widely, whereas her imports are chiefly manufactured goods and their prices are likely to be more stable. In consequence of this consideration, we might anticipate that speculation would play a less important role in the case of imports than of exports. However, it must be recognized that tariffs tend to be applied on manufactured goods at higher rates than on raw materials. Thus the influence of prospective tariff changes could have a relatively greater effect on imports. Canada's tariffs were given a major upward revision in September 1930 and were reduced, in accordance with the provisions of the Canada–U.S. Trade Agreement, at the end of 1935. Thus importers would have had a motive for importing more than they otherwise would have done prior to September 1930 and for importing less in the latter part of 1930 and the early months of 1931, and the converse would apply in 1935 and 1936. To the extent that this factor is important we would expect our figures for imports to be higher than they otherwise would have been in 1930 and 1936 and lower in 1931 and 1935.

Having completed this brief survey of possible disturbances to the postulated relationship, we turn now to consider the results of the calculations. The multiple regression equation is:

$$M = \$ -1 \cdot 50 + 0 \cdot 36 Y - 1 \cdot 02 P.$$
$$(0 \cdot 047) \ (0 \cdot 68)$$

The standard error of estimate is \$5·11, $R^2 = 0·883$, the correlation coefficient is significant at the 0·001 level, and $\bar{R} = 0·926$. The von Neumann ratio is 2·07, which does not suggest the presence of serial correlation.[4]

The values in the equation also look plausible in terms of an economic appraisal. The income coefficient is positive and less than unity as economic considerations would lead us to expect. The fact that this coefficient contains its own standard error 7·6 times makes it clear that it differs significantly from zero.

The result for the price variable is rather less satisfactory, as is invariably found to be the case in studies of this kind. For this variable there is about one chance in twelve that it is not different (in the negative direction) from zero. This does not necessarily mean that relative prices have no effect or have an unimportant influence on the volume of imports. During this period the relative variance in the fluctuations in the income variable was more than ten times that of the price variable. In the case of imports, as in the case of exports examined in Chapter 4, the fact that the income variable fluctuated relatively much more than did the price variable means that, unless the price coefficient is very much higher than seems at all probable, the effect of price fluctuations on aggregate imports will be impossible to measure with any accuracy; for this period the underlying circumstances are such that they do not give rise to data which will permit us to make a good estimate of the true value of the price coefficient. The evidence we have should not, therefore, be interpreted as implying that relative prices have little or no effect on the volume of imports. It suggests (although not at any very high level of statistical significance) that price did have an effect, but any accurate measure of this effect on imports in the aggregate is rendered impossible by the overwhelming effect of the large fluctuations in incomes in this period.

We conclude from this preliminary analysis that the regression equation is successful in meeting the various tests of statistical significance (with some necessary qualification for the coefficient of the price variable) and that the values obtained for the parameters are plausible to the economist.

We proceed now to a year-by-year comparison of the actual changes in imports with the computed changes since such an analysis may bring to light significant factors which are not evident in a more general appraisal of the type presented immediately above. The statistics are presented in Table XII.

TABLE XII
ACTUAL CHANGES, COMPUTED CHANGES, AND
RESIDUALS (PER CAPITA) FROM AGGREGATE
REGRESSION – IMPORTS

Year	Actual (M_a)	Computed (M_c)	Residual $(M_a - M_c)$
1927	\$+ 12·5	+10·3	+ 2·2
1928	+ 14·9	+11·5	+ 3·4
1929	+ 10·1	− 0·5	+10·6
1930	− 14·5	−14·0	− 0·5
1931	− 33·5	−26·5	− 7·0
1932	− 22·6	−27·5	+ 4·9
1933	− 4·6	− 3·2	− 1·4
1934	+ 5·4	+13·5	− 8·1
1935	+ 7·5	+10·9	− 3·4
1936	+ 12·4	+ 6·7	+ 5·7
1937	+ 8·4	+11·8	− 3·4
1938	− 6·0	− 3·0	− 3·0

An examination of these figures shows that in eleven of the twelve years the computed changes had the same sign as the actual changes, i.e., the estimate made from the equation gives better results than the assumption that each year's imports were unchanged from the preceding year. In only one year (1929) would the assumption of no change from the preceding year give better results than those obtained by using the regression equation.

A

Closer examination of this table reveals a tendency for the actual changes to exceed the computed changes (algebraically) in prosperous years and for the reverse relationship to appear in depressed years. In the prosperous years of the late 1920s we find imports rising more rapidly than our equation would lead us to expect.[5] In the depression years of 1930–5, we find that actual imports fell more (or rose less) than the computed change in five of the six years. And in two of the three years 1936–8, when depression was less severe than in the preceding years, actual imports showed a greater amplitude in their fluctuations than did the import values computed from our equation. This survey suggests the general conclusion that the equation may give too little weight to factors which have an expansive effect on imports in prosperous periods and similarly too little weight to factors which have a restricting effect in depressed periods.

These results are to a high degree consistent with those that our appraisal of the assumptions suggested we might expect. The discussion of the role of expectations led us to expect that imports might increase less in 1935 before the reduced tariffs came into effect and increase a bit more than indicated by the regression equation in 1936, which was the first year for the lower tariffs. Similarly, we would expect actual imports to fall a little more in 1931 after the new tariffs were in effect and to fall somewhat less than the computed value in 1930 because the higher tariffs came into effect in that year, mostly in September. In three of these four years (all except 1930), the actual experience is consistent with this pattern.

We know, too, that more restrictive attitudes and regulations in tariff administration were introduced in 1930 and that these were relaxed somewhat at the beginning of 1936, so this is consistent with the experience our review of assumptions

TABLE XIII
PERCENTAGE CHANGES IN SOME COMPONENTS OF GNE*

Expenditure components	Increase 1926 to 1929	Decrease 1929 to 1935	Increase 1935 to 1938
High import content			
Machinery and equipment	72	64	71
Consumer durables	52	32	11
Total (2 components)	62	48	32
Low import content			
Exports	7	9	11
Residential construction	7	43	28
Government	30	5	18
Consumer services	14	14	11
Total (4 components)	12	13	13

*The percentage changes were calculated from the values in constant dollars of the respective components of expenditure.

Source: Computed from *National Accounts*, Tables 5 and 48.

suggested we might expect.

The third assumption which seemed likely to give rise to some difficulty is that relating to the distribution of outlay. Here the important distinction is between the components of expenditure with a high import content and those with a low import content. Table XIII presents a summary picture of developments in this respect.

This table shows very plainly that in total, the relative fluctuations in components of expenditure with high import content was greater than for those with low import content. Among the individual components, consumer expenditure on services and exports were the least volatile items, and expenditure on machinery and equipment was consistently the most volatile. In general, this table, considered along with the pattern of residuals which we have noted from Table XII, suggests that changes in the composition of expenditure have an influence on the import relationship. A method which would give weight to the changes in the composition of expenditure would be expected to bring an improvement in the behaviour of the residuals.

Finally, we must recognize the fact that our tariff adjustment is a single factor designed to measure the price equivalent of all the tariff changes combined, but in practice tariff increases were imposed where their protective effect was expected to be greatest. Thus the restrictive effect of the tariff increases was probably underestimated with the method adopted to measure its price equivalent.

A review of these four possible sources of disturbance to our computed imports suggests that all these difficulties except that arising from the possible effects of changes in expectations could be reduced if the import total were disaggregated. This would permit groups of imports with significant common characteristics to be related to the incomes and relative prices most appropriate to them. By adding the computed imports in each group, year by year, we might expect to get a more accurate figure for total imports than that derived from the single aggregate equation.[6]

The aggregate import figure for each year was broken down into twelve subtotals: raw materials, food; raw materials, non-food; consumer durables; machinery and equipment; other manufactured metal products; manufactured textiles; other manufactured goods; freight and shipping; tourist and travel expenditure abroad; interest; dividends; and other service imports. For nine of these groups equations were calculated which were similar to the aggregate equation; in each of these equations there were two explanatory variables, one concerned with domestic expenditure and one with relative price of the imports in that group. Two of the equations (those for interest and for dividends) had no price term since price did not seem a relevant variable in these instances. For the last group, "other services," no acceptable relationship could be found and we were forced to assume that in each year expenditure for this group was unchanged from the previous year. In all eleven cases where equations were calculated they were derived, as was the aggregate equation, from the first differences of the respective time series.

This disaggregation procedure and its results are presented in more detail in Appendix G, but the most important of these results in relation to the discussion in this chapter can be summarized here. All of the eleven correlation coefficients were significant at the 0·05 level and nine (all except dividends and freight and shipping) were significant at the 0·01 level. All the income coefficients were positive and contained their own standard errors at least twice, and in nine cases the income coefficient was more than three times its own standard error.

In nine cases price variables were included in the equations. All of these were negative, and in four equations the price term was significantly different from zero – two at the 0·01 and two at the 0·05 level. The von Neumann ratio did not indicate the presence of positive serial correlation in the residuals in any of the eleven groups.

In Table xiv we show the difference between the actual year-to-year changes in imports and the sum of the changes for the twelve groups. The residuals from the aggregate regression are also given to facilitate comparisons.

TABLE XIV
SUMMARY OF RESULTS OF DISAGGREGATION – IMPORTS (all figures in 1935-9 dollars per capita)

Year	Disaggregated regressions			Residual from aggregate regression
	Actual changes (M_a)	Sum of calculated changes (M_c)	residual ($M_a - M_c$)	
1927	+12·5	+15·1	−2·6	+ 2·2
1928	+14·9	+16·9	−2·0	+ 3·4
1929	+10·1	+ 6·7	+3·4	+10·6
1930	−14·5	−12·1	−2·4	− 0·5
1931	−33·5	−24·7	−8·8	− 7·0
1932	−22·6	−27·0	+4·4	+ 4·9
1933	− 4·6	− 6·1	+1·5	− 1·4
1934	+ 5·4	+ 8·9	−3·5	− 8·1
1935	+ 7·5	+ 8·6	−1.1	− 3·4
1936	+12·4	+ 6·9	+5·5	+ 5·7
1937	+ 8·4	+ 8·4	0·0	− 3.4
1938	− 6·0	− 2·0	−4·0	− 3·0

The residuals from the disaggregated approach are, as would be expected, more satisfactory than those obtained from the aggregate equation. In the present case the actual and the sum of the computed changes in imports are of the same sign in all twelve years. The indication of bias in the residuals as between prosperous and depressed years which we noted when the aggregate equation was used is no longer apparent. Finally, the residuals are, in general, smaller than when the aggregate approach was used; the root mean square difference between the actual and the calculated changes has been reduced from $5·1 to $3·9 per capita.[7]

The conclusion from the analysis of this chapter is that both methods give results which are, in general, very satisfactory. The aggregate equation gives good estimates of the year-to-year changes in imports and of the coefficient of the income variable. It is subject to some qualification concerning the price variable, but this cannot be avoided, given the limitations in the data which are inherent in the experience of the period. There was also an indication of some bias in the residuals as between years of depression and more prosperous years.

The method based on disaggregation was substantially free of the limitations noted when the aggregate approach was used, but it did not give a fit to the data which, for the period as a whole, was greatly better than the fit obtained from the aggregate equation.

In general, the principal advantage obtained from disaggregation was to increase our confidence in the results obtained by the aggregate method. When we consider the great variety of circumstances which prevailed and the intensity of the economic disturbances of this period, the fact that such a comparatively simple regression model gives a good fit to the data not only gives empirical support to our hypothesis but, more fundamentally, provides an impressive demonstration of the potency of income and, to a lesser extent, price fluctuations in relation to the volume of current account debits in these years.

6
National Income
in Canada

In the two preceding chapters it has been shown that income in Canada was the most important factor in determining the level of imports and that income in other countries was the most important, although not the only, factor in bringing about changes in the volume of Canada's exports. It is clear that the missing link in the chain of economic causation with which we are here concerned is an explanation of the behaviour of some measure of national income in Canada. The present chapter is an attempt to supply this missing link and also to provide an empirical test of the relevant parts of the hypothesis of Chapter 1.

Before proceeding we should mention that the subject matter with which this chapter deals is of interest in its own right as well as for its relevance to this particular study. National income is the most general measure we have of economic welfare, and any investigation which throws further light, theoretical or empirical, on such a measure has its own intrinsic interest quite apart from the particular context in which it is undertaken. Since we are concerned with developing further and testing empirically our hypothesis concerning the factors which determine the behaviour of income in Canada, it is appropriate to begin with some discussion of the particular measure of national income which we shall use. For our present purposes the most satisfactory measure is the Gross National Expenditure in real terms, i.e., deflated for price changes and adjusted for changes in population and in the terms of trade. This is the measure of income that was used as an explanatory variable in the chapter on aggregate imports, and it will be convenient to use it here as well, both because the statistics have already been calculated and also because it is desirable to use the same measure of income throughout unless there are compelling reasons for doing otherwise.

There is also a reason of greater substance, in addition to the element of convenience, for using the GNE measure of income. The choice is, effectively, between using as our measure of income the Gross or the Net National Expenditure; it is not feasible to use any of the measures of national product because of the difficulty of deflating several of the items on the income side of the *National Accounts*. The difference between the Gross and the Net National Expenditure is that the former does not allow for depreciation and similar depletions of the capital stock while the latter is computed after allowance for such items has been made. Now, there is at first sight an obvious advantage in using a measure of income which provides for maintaining the capital stock intact and this consideration would lead us to favour the Net National Income as the preferred measure. But, if we adopt this definition

of income, we find that two types of difficulty arise. The first is the practical difficulty of determining the appropriate figure for depreciation, etc., at current prices
and then arriving at an adequate method of deflating it. An estimate of the figure
for depreciation is made in the *National Accounts* and this could be accepted,
although it is obvious that no such figure can be more than a good approximation
to the true value.[1] The deflation problem could be taken care of in years when net
investment was positive by deflating the net investment figure, i.e., gross investment
less depreciation, by an index of the price of capital goods. But in years in which net
investment was negative, as it was in seven of the thirteen years 1926–38,[2] this procedure is less satisfactory.[3]

The possibility that net investment may be negative in some years suggests a
problem of another sort in terms of the modern theory of income determination.
This theory distinguishes between autonomous expenditures which determine the
level of national income and induced expenditures which are determined by the level
of national income.[4] In this dichotomy investment is considered as an autonomous
item of expenditure. If we take net investment as the appropriate measure of
investment, we are assuming that replacement investment is not autonomous but
that in each year the replacement investment is just equal to the depreciation. That
this was not true in the case we are dealing with is obvious from the fact already
cited that gross investment was less than depreciation in several years of our period.
In sum, the amount of depreciation that should be provided may be largely independent of conditions in any one year, but the spending of these allowances on
replacement investment is properly regarded as an autonomous item just as is new
investment.

We conclude that we should treat gross investment rather than net investment
as an autonomous expenditure item, and, consistently with this, we consider the
Gross rather than the Net National Expenditure. By so doing we avoid a host of
difficulties at the cost of using a gross rather than a net measure of income, i.e., the
measure which we use does not provide for maintaining capital intact.

The central problem of this chapter is to test the hypothesis of Chapter 1
regarding the factors which determined the level of national income in Canada in
the 1926–38 period. This hypothesis placed much emphasis on the role of exports,
both directly and indirectly through their influence on consumption and investment. We may, therefore, begin our statistical inquiry by testing the relationship
between changes in Canada's exports of goods and services (deflated for price
changes and adjusted for changes in population) as the independent variable and
changes in the GNE (also deflated for price and population change) as the dependent variable. When this relationship has been studied, the scope of our inquiry will
be broadened to consider other possible explanations of the behaviour of the
national income in Canada in the period covered by this study.

The required figures for the GNE were calculated for the analysis of Chapter 5,
but we have not yet computed the appropriate time series for exports of goods and
services. The time series we require here will measure, in each year, the total value at
1935–9 prices of goods and services sold abroad, adjusted for changes in Canada's
population. This figure differs from that used in Chapter 4 in two respects. First, it
does not exclude exports of grains and farinaceous products because a change in

exports of these products will have an influence on income in Canada just as will changes in exports of other goods or services. In terms of the regression equations involved, in the chapter on exports it was necessary to treat exports as the dependent variable and thus we properly excluded those exports which could not be influenced to any large extent by the explanatory variables in the equation. In the present case, exports are treated as an explanatory variable exercising an influence on income. Thus fluctuations in exports, whether caused by crop variations or otherwise, would be expected to lead to fluctuations in the same direction in national income.

The second difference between the figure for exports which we require here and that required in the export chapter is that the relevant population is the population of Canada rather than that of the countries in which the exports were sold.

In order to obtain the figure required, we begin with the figure for Canada's current account credits in current dollars, as shown in the published statements for Canada's balance of international payments, and adjust the figure for freight and shipping in the years 1935–9 as described in Appendix H to put it on a consistent basis throughout our period. This figure (after adjustment for its proportionate share of residual error in the *National Accounts* in each year) was deflated with a current year weighted price index (1935–9 = 100) computed as described in Appendix H, except that in this case it was not necessary to exclude grains and farinaceous products from the index. The deflated figure was then divided by the population in each year to give the required time series of the per capita value of exports of goods and services at 1935–9 prices. The time series for GNE and for exports along with their respective first differences are shown in Table xv.

TABLE XV
ORIGINAL TIME SERIES AND FIRST DIFFERENCES FOR GNE
AND EXPORTS

Year	Original time series per capita		First differences	
	GNE	Exports	GNE	Exports
1926	$472	$136		
1927	502	132	$+30	$− 4
1928	541	146	+39	+14
1929	538	133	− 3	−13
1930	489	114	−49	−19
1931	428	99	−61	−15
1932	367	89	−61	−10
1933	351	89	−16	0
1934	387	99	+36	+10
1935	413	108	+26	+ 9
1936	433	130	+20	+22
1937	470	131	+37	+ 1
1938	463	120	− 7	−11

The general form of the regression equation in this case is:

$$Y = a + bX + u,$$

where:

Y is the GNE in real terms per capita calculated as described above.
a is the constant term in the regression equation.

X is the measure of exports of goods and services in real terms per capita calculated
as described above.

b is the calculated change in the dependent variable, Y, associated on the average
with a change of one unit in the explanatory variable, X.

u is the residual error term.

All regression equations in this chapter, as in the two preceding chapters, are
computed from the first differences of the various time series.

The simple regression of GNE on exports (which we shall designate regression I)
is found to be:

$$Y=\$2 \cdot 20+2 \cdot 21 X.$$
$$(0 \cdot 63)$$

The standard error of estimate is $24·72, $r^2=0·551$, and $\bar{r}=0·711$, which is signifi-
cant at the 0·01 level. The von Neumann ratio is 1·60, which does not indicate the
presence of serial correlation in the residuals. The residuals for each year of the
period are shown in Table XVI.

TABLE XVI
RESIDUALS* FROM REGRESSION CALCULATIONS – GNE

Year	Regression numbers			
	I	II	III	IV
1927	$+37		$+8	
1928	+ 6	$+23	−1	$− 1
1929	+24	− 2	−6	− 3
1930	−10	+ 4	+2	+ 2
1931	−30	− 6	−4	− 4
1932	−41	−20	+5	+ 3
1933	−18	0	−4	− 2
1934	+12	+20	−5	− 2
1935	+ 3	− 3	+1	+ 1
1936	−31	−30	0	− 3
1937	+33	+ 3	+7	+10
1938	+15	+11	−3	− 1

*In each case the residual is shown as the actual value of the dependent
variable less its computed value.

This regression is acceptable in terms of the standard statistical tests but, in comparison with most of the other regressions derived in this study, it suffers in two
respects. First, the coefficient of correlation, although it is significant at the 0·01
level, is not as high as for most of the other regressions. Second, the residuals show
a distinct tendency to be positive in the years of rising income and negative in the
years of falling income.

The pattern of the residuals as well as general economic considerations, as these
were developed in the hypothesis, suggest that income changes lag behind changes
in exports. In order to test this possibility regression II was computed. This regression was of the form

$$Y_t=a+b_1X_t+b_2X_{t-1}+u_t,$$

where X_t refers to the change in the export variable in year t and X_{t-1} to its change
in year $t-1$.

The regression results in this case (which we shall designate regression II) are:

$$Y_t = \$ -1 \cdot 0 + 1 \cdot 68 X_t + 1 \cdot 54 X_{t-1}.$$
$$\quad\quad\quad (0 \cdot 43) \quad (0 \cdot 44)$$

The standard error of estimate is $14·21. The coefficient of multiple correlation is significant at the 0·005 level with $R^2 = 0 \cdot 855$ and $\bar{R} = 0 \cdot 904$. The von Neumann ratio is 1·89. The residuals for individual years are shown in the second column of Table XVI.

This regression satisfies the statistical tests and gives a distinctly better fit to the data than does regression I. There is now no evidence of a cyclical pattern in the residuals, and they are, of course, smaller than for regression I.[5]

An objection may be raised that, since exports are one component of GNE, our procedure has involved correlating a total with one of its components. Consequently, another calculation was made in which the dependent variable was taken to be GNE less exports. In this case the coefficient of multiple correlation (corrected for number of degrees of freedom) is 0·832, which is significant at the 0·01 level. In other respects (except for the fact that the coefficient of X_t is reduced by 1) this regression equation is identical with regression II, as can be shown mathematically it must be if there are no rounding or other errors.

In summary, we conclude that regression II is adequate in terms of the statistical tests appropriate to this study. This means that, for the period 1926–38, it is possible to give a statistical explanation of the fluctuations in the income variable in terms of the fluctuations in the export variable for the current and the preceding year.

One very simple, though not very plausible, economic explanation of these results is that income in Canada was determined by exports and that domestic factors had no, or only a negligible, influence. This simple interpretation is subject to two objections. First, the theory of income determination requires that domestic autonomous expenditures be considered as well as exports and we have seen no reason for disputing this aspect of theory. Second, the implications of the interpretation that exports were the only cause of fluctuations in income in our case are scarcely acceptable in view of some of the findings in earlier chapters.

If we accept these results as they stand, we can infer from regression II that a change in the export variable of one unit in the current year would give rise to an increase in income of approximately 2·71 units spread over the current and the succeeding years.[6] There is difficulty in reconciling an export multiplier of this magnitude with our finding in the import chapter that the marginal prosperity to import was of the order of 0·35 to 0·40.[7] This implies a multiplier of slightly less than 3, even on the assumption that the marginal propensity to save for the economy as a whole is zero. It is improbable that the marginal propensity to save is zero, or approximately so, and it seems desirable to look for some alternative explanation of the economic implications of regression II.[8]

Such an alternative explanation, which is consistent with accepted theory, which was developed in the original hypothesis, and which meets the above objections, is that changes in income are influenced by both domestic and international factors. If this is true, the large multiplier which we found to be associated with exports in regression II is really the result of changes both in exports and in domestic factors. This suggests a new line of investigation in which both exports and the domestic determinants will appear as explanatory variables.

The domestic factors which theory requires us to consider in this context are derived from the investment and government sectors. For investment we use gross domestic investment for reasons explained earlier in this chapter. The principal difficulty here relates to the appropriate treatment of inventory changes, since such changes may be either autonomous or induced, and in any given situation some part of the change is likely to be autonomous and some induced.[9] There is no satisfactory way of separating the two types of change, and we have arbitrarily classified the total as autonomous. In this case, as in others where somewhat arbitrary decisions cannot be avoided, the ultimate test comes in the performance of the model in which such decisions are incorporated.

The figure for domestic investment, including changes in non-farm business inventories in current dollars, can be readily calculated from the *National Account*. Each component, except inventory change, was deflated with the implicit price index (converted to the base 1935–9 =100) for that component. Inventory changes were deflated with the index of wholesale prices. The sum of these deflated components was then adjusted for changes in the terms of trade,[10] the proportionate share of residual error was allocated to it, and it was deflated with the population figure in each year to give the required time series for domestic investment. Similar adjustments for changes in the terms of trade, the share of residual error, and for population were made in each of the domestic components used in any regression analysis in this chapter.

From the government sector the figure we use is the net deficit of governments. Here the choice is effectively between this measure and total government spending. Tests were made with both measures, and from these it appeared clear that the net

TABLE XVII
ORIGINAL TIME SERIES AND FIRST DIFFERENCES FOR INVESTMENT
AND GOVERNMENT DEFICIT

	Original time series per capita			First differences*		
Year	Investment	Gov't deficit	Investment plus gov't deficit	Investment (V)	Gov't deficit (G)	D = V+G
1926	$ 84	$−4	$ 80			
1927	100	−3	97	$+16	$+1	$+17
1928	113	−6	107	+13	−3	+10
1929	120	+1	121	+7	+7	+14
1930	85	+20	105	−35	+19	−16
1931	51	+31	82	−34	+10	−24
1932	18	+29	47	−33	−2	−35
1933	17	+20	37	−1	−9	−10
1934	32	+20	52	+15	0	+15
1935	38	+19	57	+6	−1	+5
1936	40	+5	45	+2	−14	−12
1937	56	+5	61	+17	0	+17
1938	53	+15	68	−3	+10	+7

*The first differences were computed from original time series calculated to one decimal place. The figures have been rounded to the nearest whole number here with the result that in a few cases the first differences differ by 1 from the value indicated by the original time series shown above.

deficit was preferable. Since this is also the measure that is most frequently used in such cases as this, we have used it in this study.[11]

The current dollar measure of the net deficit (a surplus is treated as a negative deficit) of governments is available from the *National Accounts*. There is no obvious price deflator to use for this measure but, because government economic activities cover such a wide variety of transactions, we use the implicit price deflator for the GNE (determined by dividing the value of the GNE at current prices by its value at 1935–9 prices) as the index with the broadest coverage.

The time series for gross domestic investment, for the deficit of governments (both adjusted as required for our purposes), and for the sum of the two and the required first differences are shown in Table XVII.

We wish now to test the hypothesis that the changes in GNE (Y) can be explained in terms of the changes in exports (X) and changes in the sum of the two domestic factors (gross domestic investment and the deficit of governments, which we shall designate by D). A multiple regression of Y on X and D was calculated. The equation is:

$$Y = \$2 \cdot 87 + 1 \cdot 59X + 1 \cdot 50D.$$
$$(0 \cdot 13) \quad (0 \cdot 094)$$

The standard error of estimate is $4·55, and the coefficient of multiple correlation is significant at the 0·001 level with $R^2 = 0 \cdot 985$ and $\bar{R} = 0 \cdot 991$. The von Neumann ratio is 2·46. The residuals from this equation (regression III) are shown in the third column of Table XVI. Again, as for regression II, there is no indication of a cyclical pattern in the residuals and, in eight of the eleven years for which comparison is possible, the residuals are smaller (ignoring the signs) than are the residuals for the same years when regression II is used.[12]

This regression is more satisfactory, both because the coefficient of correlation is higher and because the standard errors of the parameters are a smaller fraction of the parameters themselves than for regression II. We conclude that regression III is to be preferred to regression II on the basis both of the statistical tests and of the underlying economic theory.

In considering the hypothesis that the GNE was determined by exports alone we found (regression II) that matters were substantially improved if we included exports in the preceding year as an additional explanatory variable. To extend this approach to the present case we would need to add two additional explanatory variables – exports in the preceding year and domestic factors (D) in the preceding year. This would not only reduce the number of degrees of freedom, but it would almost certainly lead to serious difficulties with multicollinearity among the explanatory variables.

A preferable alternative approach is to use the change in income in the preceding year as the additional explanatory variable. This variable will reflect the influence of a broader range of effects, i.e., changes in sectors other than those represented by our two explanatory variables, X and D. It will also take into account changes which occurred prior to period $t-1$ to the extent that they influenced GNE in period $t-1$. Consequently, regression IV was calculated. It is identical with regression III except that GNE in period $t-1$ was added as a third explanatory variable. The regression equation is:

$$Y = \$1 \cdot 81 + 1 \cdot 67X + 0 \cdot 038Y_{t-1} + 1 \cdot 34D.$$
$$\quad\quad\quad (0 \cdot 10) \quad (0 \cdot 14) \quad\quad\; (0 \cdot 10)$$

The standard error of estimate is $3·23$. The coefficient of multiple correlation is significant at the $0·001$ level, $R^2 = 0·992$, and $\bar{R} = 0·995$. The von Neumann ratio is $3·15$, and in the residuals there is no evidence of a cyclical pattern.[13] (The residuals are shown in the last column of Table XVI.)

Objection may be raised to regressions III and IV, as to the previous ones, because we have related changes in the expenditure variable to changes in explanatory variables which are themselves components of expenditure. This objection is more serious for regressions III and IV than it was for regressions I and II because for the two former regressions the explanatory variable includes changes in gross domestic investment as well as changes in exports, and the two together might very well account for a substantial part of the changes in total expenditure.

In order to deal with this point, two additional calculations were made which correspond to regressions III and IV respectively. In each case the components of expenditure which were included as explanatory variables were excluded from the dependent variable (GNE). The coefficient of multiple correlation, corrected for degrees of freedom, was found to be $0·910$ for the case corresponding to regression III and $0·952$ for that corresponding to regression IV. Each of these coefficients is significant at the $0·001$ level.

In this chapter we have presented the results of four regression analyses, each of which represented a particular formulation of the hypothesis concerning the factors responsible for determining the level of GNE in Canada in the period with which this study deals. All four regressions met the standard statistical tests at the conventional levels, but regression I was distinctly less satisfactory than any of the others. Since regression I attempted to explain changes in GNE solely in terms of changes in current exports, it is surprising that it gave results which were as satisfactory as they were found to be. However, compared with the other three regressions, regression I fares badly, and we conclude that for most purposes this simple approach is not adequate.

Regression II, in which the explanatory variables are current exports and exports in the preceding year, satisfies the statistical criteria at levels substantially more exacting than those which are conventionally employed. Since it uses only exports (current and in the preceding year) as explanatory variables it serves to emphasize the importance of exports to the Canadian economy, a point which was stressed in the hypothesis of Chapter 1.

Regression III (which uses current exports and current domestic investment plus the government deficit as explanatory variables) meets the standard statistical tests at still higher levels than does regression II, and it is also more adequate in terms of the underlying economic theory.

Regression IV contains the same two explanatory variables as does regression III, and in addition it has, as an additional explanatory variable, the change in GNE in the preceding year. Since regression III satisfied the statistical criteria at such high levels, there is little room for further improvement, but in fact regression IV, judged by these criteria, is preferable. In addition, by including the prior year's change in GNE as an additional explanatory variable, provision is made for the delayed effect of events which occurred in the more distant past to the extent that these are relevant. On the other hand, it has two degrees of freedom fewer than has regression III, and it may be questioned whether the improvement in the equation is worth the loss of these degrees of freedom.

It is also worth drawing attention to the stability of the coefficient of the export term in regressions II, III, and IV. In these three regressions the value of this parameter varies within the narrow range 1·59 to 1·68. Moreover, if we take any one of these three values and take a range equal to one standard error of that value on either side of it we will include both the other two values. This stability is another indication of the importance of the export factor since, if it were not so important, the value of its coefficient as determined from these equations would be subject to greater disturbance from fluctuations in other factors.

Comments similar to those above would apply also to the regressions which were computed from the percentage changes in the same variables. In each case, however, the results described in the text were slightly better than the corresponding results derived from the percentage first differences.

We conclude that our hypothesis concerning the factors which were responsible for fluctuations in Canada's GNE in the period covered by this study has withstood the empirical tests satisfactorily. In addition, there is some reason to think that the general hypothesis which we have investigated in this study will be found to be relevant,[14] possibly after some modification in detail, to the circumstances of more recent years.

7
Conclusion

Our purpose here is to draw together the results of the analysis reported in the preceding chapters and to make a general assessment of the original hypothesis in the light of the empirical findings.

Our original hypothesis, which was developed in Chapter 1 and summarized at the end of that chapter, was that cyclical disturbances in a dependent resource economy would tend to reach it through the current account credits in its balance of payments, rather than to be initiated by domestic factors or through the capital account of the balance of payments. The expected sequence of events, in causal but not necessarily in chronological order, was: an increase in incomes in countries in which the products of the dependent resource economy found their major markets; a consequent increase in exports from the dependent resource economy to these countries; an increase in incomes in the export industries, the spending of which would increase incomes throughout the economy; increased investment induced by the increased demand in both the domestic and the export industries; an induced increase in consumption brought about by the combined effect of these expansionist factors; and, as a result of the increase in aggregate demand in the dependent resource economy, an increase in its imports. When the expansion in external demand ceased, it was anticipated that the process would operate in reverse to bring about a contraction in exports, domestic investment, consumption, and imports. This, stripped to its essentials, is the hypothesis which has been under consideration in Chapters 2 to 6.

The first two of these chapters dealt with certain preliminary matters in order to clear the way for the actual testing of the hypothesis, which is the business of Chapters 4, 5, and 6. In Chapter 2 it was established that in the period 1926–38 Canada had the characteristics of a dependent resource economy as such an economy was defined in Chapter 1. Canada's current account credits accounted directly for one-quarter, or slightly more, of the GNE; and, more relevantly for our purposes, fluctuations in Canada's current account credits were found, on the average, to be almost one-third of the fluctuations in the GNE. On the other hand, Canada's trade and fluctuations in it were a small proportion (of the order of 5 per cent) of the corresponding total figures for the world. That Canada was also a resource economy, i.e., that she had a high ratio of natural resources, and especially of undeveloped natural resources, to population, was shown by the evidence that Canada was astonishingly well supplied in relation to her population with almost all the natural resources (tin and bauxite being the only exceptions of any consequence) which are generally considered to be of major importance. The undeveloped natural resources at the end of the period were shown, by reference to postwar developments, to have been abundant in relation to Canada's population.

Having dealt, in Chapter 2, with the relevant structural characteristics of the economy, we turned in Chapter 3 to consider its cyclical behaviour in our period. As a single simple measure of the degree of prosperity or depression in the economy in any year we used the extent to which the non-agricultural GNE at 1935–9 prices fell short of what a full employment GNE, also measured at 1935–9 prices, would have been in each year. This provided a record which shows that, after falling somewhat short of full employment in 1926 and 1927, the economy came very close to full employment in 1928 and 1929, although it probably did not quite reach that state in either of those years. Unemployment increased sharply after 1929, and in 1933 the actual non-agricultural GNE had fallen to between 36 and 40 per cent below the full employment level. Recovery proceeded slowly until 1937, but even in this year, the peak peacetime recovery year of the late 1930s, the non-agricultural GNE was between 23 and 30 per cent below full employment. In 1938 the magnitude of unemployment increased again.

This record of the prosperity and depression in the economy brings to light three aspects which are relevant to our inquiry. First, it shows that in the period the economy experienced the vicissitudes of economic fortune varying from a condition approaching (but probably falling just slightly short of) full employment in 1928 and 1929 to very acute depression in the early 1930s. Second, it shows that the expansion which reached its peak in 1937 fell far short of reaching the full employment position. Third, our measure of unemployment in terms of the loss of income entailed as a percentage of a full employment income gives a substantially greater figure than is indicated if we take the average percentage of the working force reported in the official statistics as being "without jobs and seeking work" in a given year.

The actual statistical testing of the hypothesis is carried out for the aggregates in Chapters 4 to 6. Appendices F and G, which are supplementary to Chapters 4 and 5, are concerned with the disaggregation of the exports and imports, respectively. In the paragraphs below we shall begin with some general observations concerning the methodology used in these three chapters and the related appendices. Following these observations, a summary and appraisal of the tests of the hypothesis will be given.

In testing the hypothesis it has been necessary to be rigorous in order to ensure that the tests were adequate. This rigour may be discussed with reference to the data which were used and to the methods employed in dealing with them. The three variables whose behaviour we are attempting to explain are current account credits, GNE in Canada, and current account debits. For each of these we have included the value in every year of the period and we have also included all the components of the total except in cases where there were good *a priori* reasons for excluding some part of the total.[1] Thus, in the chapters on exports and imports our general principle was to include total current account credits and total current account debits and not commodity trade only. For imports it was possible to achieve this objective, but for exports it was obviously necessary, in view of the demonstrated large

c

fluctuations in crop yields which are independent of economic conditions, to exclude exports of grains and farinaceous products. There is also a case for excluding exports of non-monetary gold, but, for reasons which appear to be in large measure fortuitous, this turned out to be unnecessary. In Appendix E we have given the regression equation for exports, excluding both non-monetary gold and grains and farinaceous products.

The GNE, the third of the three variables whose behaviour we have investigated, is also included in its entirety except for the very minor exclusion of changes in inventories on farms. This procedure has been recommended by other writers, and it seems clear, for reasons explained in Chapters 5 and 6, that it is appropriate for our purposes. Apart from these few exceptions, each of which has been justified on *a priori* grounds, the testing of the hypothesis has been applied to all current account credits, to all GNE and to all current account debits, for all the years of the period 1926–38.[2]

We have also been consistent throughout in our method of using the data. For total expenditure or for any of its components we have used the value at 1935–9 prices, adjusted for changes in population. In each case, too, the value at current prices has been deflated with a current year weighted price index.[3]

The price and cost variables, all of which are ratios between price indexes, have been calculated throughout from base year weighted price indexes except for a few minor cases in which current year weighted indexes were the only ones available.[4]

The form of the regression was also kept symmetrical with respect to the export and import equations. In both cases the explanatory variables were income (in real terms, adjusted for population change) and relative prices. In the export equation it was necessary to add a supply factor because Canada's supply of exports could not be taken to be perfectly elastic relative to the rest of the world. The analogous term was not required in the import equation because it is appropriate to assume that the supply of imports to Canada from the rest of the world is perfectly elastic.

Finally, all the regression equations were computed from the first differences of the respective time series. This technique is used, for reasons discussed in Appendix A, in order to deal with certain statistical problems which are likely to be encountered if the original data are used. The regressions reported in the text are all derived from the simple first differences of the various series, but all the important aggregate regressions were also calculated for percentage changes in the variables. In every case the evaluation of the results of the regression for the simple first differences which is reported in the text would apply without significant change to the regression based on the percentage first differences.

It is now time to bring together the results of the regression analyses and to compare the empirical results obtained with the original hypothesis. There are three major sections to the hypothesis which deal, respectively, with exports, GNE, and imports. We shall appraise the elements of our hypothesis in this order rather than in the order in which the three corresponding chapters appear in this study. Since all the regression calculations are based on first differences, and since the hypothesis can equally well be considered in terms of changes, it is to be assumed that in the discussion which follows we are referring to *changes* in the values of the various measures rather than to their absolute levels.

The first part of our hypothesis is that Canada's current account credits will fluctuate in sympathy with incomes in other countries. When this aspect of the hypothesis was considered in more detail in Chapter 4, it was found necessary to exclude exports of grains and farinaceous products. It was also found desirable to include a factor to take into account the price of Canada's exports of goods and services relative to prices in the importing countries and a factor on the supply side to relate costs of production in Canada to the prices of Canada's exports.

The regression analysis of the hypothesis, modified as described in the foregoing paragraph, gave very satisfactory results. The coefficient of correlation was found to be significant at the 0·001 level, and the income term was almost five times as large as its own standard error. Both the price and the supply terms in the equation had the appropriate sign, but neither was different from zero at the 0·05 level of significance. The regression equation as a whole was found to explain 91 per cent of the fluctuations in exports. Some 70 per cent of all fluctuations in exports was explained by the income term; the supply factor was next in importance and accounted for about 15 per cent.

In Appendix F a separate regression was calculated for exports to the United States. The results in this case do not differ in any major respect from those obtained in the aggregate case although income is found to be relatively an even more important factor for exports to the United States than for total exports.

The second major element in our hypothesis explains the behaviour of GNE in Canada in terms of the behaviour of Canada's current account credits. It was found possible, by taking into account, as explanatory variables, exports in the current year and exports in the preceding year to obtain a regression equation which satisfied all the standard statistical tests at conventionally accepted levels and, in some respects, at more exacting levels. It was found that an equation which also met all the standard tests and did so at even higher levels was obtained when we included the sum of gross domestic investment and the deficits of governments as a second explanatory variable rather than exports in the prior year. The marked improvement in the equation which this substitution brings about suggests that there is a larger element of autonomy in the domestic factors than was implied by the hypothesis.[5] But, when the hypothesis is modified to take into account the domestic factors as autonomous elements in the regression, all the standard statistical tests are satisfied at levels of significance which are much above those that are conventionally required in work of this type, e.g., the regression equation accounts for 98 per cent of the fluctuations in GNE.

The third, and final, major aspect of our hypothesis is that changes in GNE in Canada will be accompanied by changes in current account debits in the same direction. We included relative prices of imports in the regression equation as a second explanatory variable since this was suggested by theoretical economic considerations. The aggregate regression satisfied all the standard statistical tests except that the coefficient of the price term, while it had the appropriate negative sign, did not differ from zero at the 0·05 level of significance. In all other respects the equation was satisfactory and accounted for 88 per cent of the fluctuations in imports.

Further confirmation of this third aspect of our hypothesis is provided in

Appendix G, in which the aggregate current account debits are disaggregated into twelve separate groups. For only one of the twelve groups ("all other current account debits") is the coefficient of correlation found to be lower than required for significance at the 0·05 level and, in nine cases, it is significant at the 0·01 level or better. In addition, for all seven of the commodity groups, the price term is negative, and is significantly different from zero at the 0·05 level for four groups. The income variable is found to be significantly different from zero at the 0·01 level or better for three of the five service groups.

This concludes the assessment of the three elements in our hypothesis, and this assessment in turn prompts four observations which seem of general application concerning it. First, the hypothesis was not contradicted by any of the tests we have made. Second, it requires amendment to provide for price effects in both the export and the import equations and also for supply effects in the export equation. In our period these factors were very much secondary to income in their effects on the respective dependent variables, but in other periods in which relative fluctuations in prices might be greater and fluctuations in income might be relatively smaller the failure to include such price factors could be more serious. Third, we must make special allowance for variables which are largely influenced by non-economic factors. Of these, the most important example is provided by exports of grains and farinaceous products. Fourth, it appears that it is preferable to put somewhat more emphasis on domestic autonomous factors than was implied in our hypothesis. With these modifications our original hypothesis was found to provide an explanation of the relationships involved which was acceptable in terms of its economic content and which withstood the statistical tests very well.

8
Postscript on Implications
for Economic Policy

The emphasis in this study has been on the development and statistical testing of an hypothesis rather than on questions of economic policy. But it would be disappointing if no conclusions for policy were to emerge from this lengthy investigation, especially since the original project was suggested by the major problem of economic policy in the period under consideration. This concluding chapter is, then, intended to draw attention to, and explore briefly, some of the implications for policy which are suggested by our findings in earlier chapters.

Our empirical investigations have dealt, apart from a few minor points in Chapters 2 and 3, with the interwar period and so it might appear that our conclusions, and the policy implications related to them, would be relevant only to that period. In a very strict sense this is true but, in practice, the general implications for the interwar period seem likely to be at least broadly true for the postwar period as well. The basic hypothesis was developed for a resource economy which was very much exposed to the changes in economic circumstances beyond its borders but which did not itself have much effect on economic conditions in the rest of the world. This description applies to postwar Canada as well as to the Canadian economy of the earlier period and so the theory should still be relevant. That this is true is suggested by the fact that the analysis of cyclical fluctuations in Canada developed both by the Royal Commission on Banking and Finance[1] and by the Royal Commission on Taxation[2] is consistent with our treatment of these matters. It is, therefore, reasonable to expect that the broad conclusions on policy questions that emerge from our study will be relevant to more recent periods.

The general features of the Canadian economy relevant to this study appear to be not essentially different now compared with what they were before World War II; the principal difference would seem to lie not in any fundamental change in the nature of the economy, but rather in the nature of the economic problems to which it has been subject. For most of the earlier period, the policy question of all-consuming interest was how to alleviate the problems of depression. Since the war we have had periods of serious underemployment, but problems of this nature have been neither so severe nor so prolonged as in the 1930s. On the other hand, difficulties of overfull employment did not arise significantly in the interwar period, but they have on more than one occasion given rise to difficulties in the postwar years. In addition, it appears that prices have become less flexible downward and that they tend to increase more readily than in the earlier period. This "ratchet effect" can be attributed partly, but not entirely, to more buoyant conditions of demand. Thus, to the extent that policy problems are those of inadequate demand, we may reasonably hope that our analysis in earlier chapters will be relevant to them; to the extent that the problems are those of inflation, it seem probable that our conclusions will be less relevant.

THE ECONOMIC COST OF UNEMPLOYMENT

In our discussion of unemployment in Chapter 3 we concluded it would be reasonable to consider an annual average unemployment figure of $3\frac{1}{2}$ per cent of the non-agricultural labour force as consistent with "full employment." This figure is somewhat higher than that which has been achieved under non-inflationary conditions in a number of other countries and, even after making due allowance for the greater importance of seasonal factors deriving from variations in climatic conditions in Canada than in many other countries, it seems that, as an *ideal*, this $3\frac{1}{2}$ per cent figure is too high. Some allowance for seasonal and frictional unemployment is obviously necessary, but we wish here to suggest the possibility of reducing this figure and the economic and social advantages to be realized from such a reduction.

Why should this figure be as high as it is? It appears that at least a part of the answer is to be found in the influence of both regional and seasonal factors. In 1966, for example, unemployment over the year averaged 3·6 per cent of the labour force (and just under 4 per cent of the non-agricultural labour force) and so, on the basis of this and other evidence,[3] it seems appropriate to treat 1966 as a year which came close to, but probably did not quite reach, full employment. In Ontario, in the same year, unemployment averaged only 2·5 per cent and varied from a high of 3·3 per cent in January to a low of 1·8 per cent in October.[4] The corresponding figures for the Atlantic provinces are an annual average of 6·4 per cent with a high of 10·9 and a low of 3·7 per cent.[5] The average unemployment figure for the other regions (except for the prairie provinces, where it was slightly below the Ontario level[6]) was between the level in Ontario and that in the Atlantic provinces.

In the light of these evidences of seasonal and regional unemployment[7] in 1966 it would seem a reasonable objective (over a period of years) to reduce the average annual percentage unemployment for the country as a whole from 3·5 to 2·5 per cent of the non-agricultural labour force. This would imply, for the labour force of 1966, an increase in the number employed at full employment of some 70,000 persons or, to put the matter in relative terms, a reduction of more than 25 per cent in the number unemployed. The increase in GNP would be of the order of $500 million.[8]

These magnitudes are large, but the social benefits would be even greater than these calculations suggest because they would be heavily concentrated on those regions, age groups, and occupations where the incidence of unemployment is greatest. It would, of course, require time to achieve this position but the evidence suggests that it is a reasonable objective of policy. The social, as well as the purely economic, benefits to be derived from the successful implementation of such a policy are sufficiently great that it would be worth a major effort to realize it.[9]

MAINTAINING THE LEVEL OF INVESTMENT

We have seen in our analysis that, although exports seem to have been the principal autonomous factor in relation to fluctuations in income, domestic investment has also played a part of some significance. There have been periods, both in the 1930s and in the postwar years, when there was weakness in the investment sector and when a substantial contribution to national prosperity could have been made by a successful policy of maintaining investment at a level closer to the proportion borne to GNE under conditions of full employment. We shall examine this matter first for 1937, the most prosperous peacetime year in the later 1930s, and shall then turn to consider the position in 1961, the postwar year in which unemployment as a percentage of the labour force reached its highest level.

Examination of the statistics for 1937 suggests that there was in that year an attractive field for desirable measures of public policy in the area of investment. This is especially true in the area of non-residential construction, particularly for governments and public utilities. There are a number of considerations which point to this conclusion, and which can be brought to light by comparing the economic position of the Canadian economy in 1937 with its position in 1929. In order to make this comparison effectively, both here and in other parts of this discussion on economic policy, it is desirable to deal with the *levels* of different economic magnitudes rather than with *changes in levels* which, for technical and statistical reasons, have been our concern in most chapters of this study.

The feature common to both 1929 and 1937 is that in each of these two years there was a cyclical peak, but for our present purposes we are more interested in the fact that 1929 was a year in which full employment was closely approached, if it was not actually reached, while in 1937 the GNE was some 27 per cent below the full employment level.[10]

When we come to examine the circumstances in these two years in more detail we look first (in view of our findings in Chapter 6) at the level of exports and at the domestic factors, gross domestic investment and the net deficit of governments. We find that current account credits (at constant prices and in per capita terms as shown in Table xv) in both 1936 and 1937 were almost exactly equal to the 1929 level. The government deficit was slightly larger (Table xvii) in both 1936 and 1937 than in 1929, but gross domestic investment in 1937 was less than one-half of the 1929 level. These figures tend, incidentally, to support our conclusion in Chapter 6 that there were important influences in addition to exports which affected domestic investment.

One possible explanation for the low level of domestic investment which might be considered is that, because prices were lower in 1937 than in 1929, business was less profitable, and so investment was depressed. In fact, however, corporation profits both before and after taxes were higher, in current dollars, in 1937 than they were in 1929; and this would be true, *a fortiori*, if we were to consider the purchasing power of business profits.[11]

Further investigation reveals that the component of investment which was lowest in 1937 compared with 1929 was non-residential construction; at constant prices this component of investment was only 41 per cent of the 1929 level. The corresponding figures for the other components are 79 per cent for residential construction, 64 per cent for machinery and equipment, and 82 per cent for changes in non-farm business inventories.[12] Of this decline in non-residential construction, approximately one-half was represented by the decline in investment in public utilities.[13]

To put the point more directly, it appears that approximately one-quarter of the decline in gross domestic investment in 1937 compared with 1929 was represented by the decline in public utility construction. Since both exports and the government deficit were at approximately the same level in these two years, it would seem that a major contribution to economic stability could have been made if it had been possible to stabilize investment in non-residential construction, and especially in public utility construction, at a high level.

It is impossible to give any accurate quantitative measure of the effect on national income of maintaining non-residential construction in 1937 at the 1929 level, but a crude estimate of the general order of magnitude may be of some interest. If this objective could have been realized, investment would have been increased by something less than $400 million and, allowing for multiplier effects, income could have been expected to rise by perhaps $500–600 million. This would have increased GNE by a figure approaching 10 per cent and would have reduced the shortfall of GNE below its full employment level by one-quarter to one-third.

The policy would also have been attractive in that its success would not seem likely to have led to balance of payments difficulties. The import content of expenditure on non-residential construction tends to be rather lower than it is in many other areas of expenditure and so the danger of balance of payments difficulties would be reduced. And, of course, the multiplier effects on domestic income would have been increased accordingly. In fact, there was a current account surplus of almost $200 million in 1937 and so it seems highly improbable that the policy would have encountered a limitation arising from balance of payments considerations. Finally, we observe that the direct impact of such a policy would have brought benefit to the construction industry, which was especially hard hit by the depression.

There were very great differences in many respects between the economic circumstances of 1937 and those of 1961, but a feature which is common to both years is that the relatively low level of domestic investment was a major source of economic weakness. The year 1961 was, as we have already noted, the most depressed year of the postwar period and the most serious weakness in that year was in private investment. This is illustrated in Table XVIII, which shows the major constituents of GNE in each of the years 1956, 1961, and 1966 as a percentage of GNE. Both 1956 and 1966 were years in which full employment was either actually achieved or closely approached and so the figures for them are useful as giving some indication of the distribution of outlay which could be expected under conditions of full employment and as suggesting how the composition of outlay in 1961 differed from what might have been expected if there had been full employment in that year.

The most conspicuous feature of Table XVIII is the difference between the percentage distribution of the major constituent items of GNE in 1956 and 1966 compared with 1961. In 1961, the depressed year, we notice that investment was a substantially smaller proportion of GNE than it was in either 1956 or 1966. We also notice that in these two prosperous years the percentage distribution of the items in Table XVIII was very similar.

TABLE XVIII
COMPONENTS OF GNE AS PERCENTAGE OF TOTAL GNE

	1956	1961	1966
Personal expenditure on consumer goods and services	61·6	65·3	60·3
Government expenditure on goods and services	17·6	19·3	19·3
Business gross fixed capital formation plus value of physical change in inventories non-farm	24·8	18·6	22·8
Exports of goods and services	20·8	20·4	22·3
Imports of goods and services	−25·2	−22·8	−24·2
Residual error of estimate	−0·5	—	−0·5
GNE	100·0	100·0	100·0

Sources: *National Accounts*, 1962, 22 and *ibid.*, 1967, 15.

When we examine the behaviour of the investment item we find that the total, including inventory changes, showed a downward trend in the period 1956 to 1961 and that, by 1961, the figure was some 20 per cent below the 1956 figure.[14] All the other major constituents of expenditure showed an upward trend and by 1961 the total for all other items of GNE combined was more than 20 per cent higher than in 1956.[15] And, just as investment was the weakest constituent of expenditure in the period 1956 to 1961, it showed the greatest percentage rate of increase in the succeeding five-year period so that by 1966 it had moved about two-thirds of the distance toward regaining the relative importance which it had had ten years earlier.[16]

It is apparent that investment was the least buoyant of the major items of GNE in the first five years of the period shown in Table XVIII. It is tempting to try to quantify the contribution of this weakness in the investment sector to the depressed conditions of 1961 and we can do this if we are prepared to make assumptions concerning what the distribution of expenditure would have been in 1961 if there had been full employment in that year. The assumption we shall make for purposes of this calculation is that, if there had been full employment in 1961, the percentage importance of the various major components of GNE would have been equal to the average of the 1956 and the 1966 percentage figure for each.

In Table XIX we have estimated the full employment GNE in 1961 by taking the actual figure from the National Accounts and applying to it the factor suggested by the reports of the Economic Council of Canada.[17] This total is then distributed as suggested in the preceding paragraph and from this figure we determine the extent to which the actual expenditure on each item fell short of the calculated full employment level.

If we consider the four major expenditure items (consumption, government, investment, and exports) we find that the total shortfall was $5·3 billion and, of this, $3·3 billion or 62 per cent was attributed to investment while only 23 per cent arose in the export sector. We need to recall the assumptions concerning the full employment distribution of expenditure on which these calculations are based but, even

C*

after allowing for any reasonable margin of error here, there can be no doubt that a large percentage of the deficiency of aggregate demand in 1961 is attributable to investment. On our assumptions domestic investment was the major source of weakness in the economy in 1961.

TABLE XIX
DISTRIBUTION OF CONSTITUENTS OF GNE – ACTUAL COMPARED WITH
CALCULATED FULL EMPLOYMENT FIGURES (all dollar figures in billions)

	Constituent of GNE as % of total at full employment	Calculated amount at full employment	Actual amount of each item in 1961	Deficiency of actual below full employment level
Personal expenditure on consumer goods and services	61·0	$25·0	$24·5	$0·5
Government expenditure on goods and services	18·5	7·5	7·2	0·3
Business gross fixed capital formation plus value of physical change in inventories	24·2	10·0	6·7	3·3
Exports of goods and services	21·5	8·8	7·6	1·2
Total of items above	125·2%	$51·3	$46·0	$5·3
Imports of goods and services	−24·7	−10·1	−8·5	−1·6
Residual error	−0·5	−0·2	*	−0·2
GNE	100·0%	$41·0	$37·5	$3·5

*Less than $50 million.

Sources: Table XVIII and *National Accounts*, 1967, Table 2.

We have now examined in some detail two years which are separated by almost a quarter of a century and for which the economic circumstances differ in many respects. In particular, unemployment in 1937 was much more serious than it was in 1961 and, partly as a consequence of this, the balance of payments was in surplus in 1937 whereas there was a large deficit in 1961. Notwithstanding these marked differences between the two years in question, they have in common the fact that the proximate cause of economic difficulty in both cases was weakness in the investment sector.

This conclusion is not inconsistent with our hypothesis concerning the role of exports in the economic process, but it does add further support to our earlier conclusion that domestic investment is, to an appreciable extent, independent of exports and that policy should give adequate recognition of this fact.

SOME GENERAL IMPLICATIONS OF THIS STUDY

In the foregoing sections of this chapter we have been concerned with exploring in a quantitative sense some of the areas to which our attention had been attracted by facts revealed in the course of investigating the general hypothesis. In this section we shall proceed from our general hypothesis to its implications for policy in specific areas, but we shall be more interested in the relevance for policy in general rather than in the details of a particular historical episode.

A principal theme in this study has been that Canada, with her abundant supplies of natural resources, has been able to attract from abroad net capital inflows which permitted economic development to proceed more rapidly than would have been possible on the basis of domestic savings alone. And, as an implication of this, we have noted the tendency for Canada's current account balance of payments to deteriorate in times of increasing prosperity and to become stronger in periods of rising unemployment. There are a number of implications of this hypothesis which it seems worthwhile to mention and discuss briefly in the remainder of this chapter.

1   Investment and Resource Allocation

The fact that, in prosperous times, investment in Canada draws on outside sources of capital as well as on domestic savings leads to a situation in which investment tends to be a high proportion of GNE.[18] This, in turn, has implications for the allocation of factors because, for many types of investment and especially construction (which accounts for more than half of total capital investment), a large part of the resources must, for technological reasons, come from domestic sources. This high concentration of resources in the capital goods industries is made possible by Canada's ability to borrow abroad and this is indeed an essential part of the mechanism by which Canada's foreign borrowing of financial capital is converted into physical capital. Thus in periods of prosperity we find that an unusually high proportion of domestic resources are found in the capital goods industries and especially in the construction industry. Later, when the boom has ended, there will be a reduction in demand for resources in these industries and some movement out of these industries will (in the absence of public policy measures which succeed in maintaining investment) be appropriate.

Two implications for policy are suggested by this line of thought. The first is the importance in such circumstances of adopting measures which will increase the mobility of resources into and out of the capital goods industries. If resources are made more mobile, it will require both less time and also a smaller price or wage incentive to cause factors to move into the investment sector. This will reduce delays and will also help to keep down capital costs. Later, when the boom has ended, it is desirable that resources be mobile out of these industries.

It is easy to see and obvious to suggest that increased mobility would be desirable but there are many barriers, economic, psychological, and sociological, to any substantial increases in mobility. Even under the most favourable circumstances no more than a modest increase in mobility is likely to be realized. One of the barriers in times of contraction and depression is the fact that, when capital investment is declining and thus resources should be moving out of the investment sector, it is highly probable that other sectors of the economy will be contracting as well and so alternative employment opportunities will not be easily found. Increased mobility is desirable in both expansion and contraction periods, but in the latter case there is also need for some measures to maintain demand after the investment boom has reached its peak and begun to decline.

2 *Foreign Exchange Reserves*

In the circumstances described relative to the cyclical pattern of the balance of payments there is a special need to build up the country's foreign exchange reserves as the boom moves toward full employment (and, given the favourable domestic economic situation at such a time, it is likely to be possible to do this). As the boom proceeds, the current account balance typically becomes more passive and the capital inflows increase. After the downturn the level of national income falls, either absolutely or in relation to its long-term trend value, and there is likely to be a corresponding change in the amount of domestic savings which are available. But capital projects require time to complete and, in addition, there is likely to be a lag between the upper turning point of the cycle and the associated reduction in consumption spending. The result of this is that the passive current account balance is likely to increase in the period immediately after the downturn. Later, if the contraction is not reversed, capital projects will have been completed and consumption adjusted to a level more appropriate to the less prosperous circumstances of the economy and in this stage there is likely to be a sharp reduction in imports and a marked strengthening in the current account balance.

Since the current account balance is likely to be heavily passive in the period just after the downturn, it is most desirable in such circumstances to have large foreign exchange reserves in order to avoid the necessity of adopting policies which would exacerbate an already difficult situation. If this balance of payments difficulty were expected to persist for longer than the period of adjustment mentioned above, there might be no means of avoiding policy measures designed to strengthen the country's balance of payments position. But in Canada's case the difficulties are likely to be relatively short-lived and so, provided means can be found to see the country through this period of adjustment, these undesirable measures can probably be avoided altogether and the contraction made correspondingly less severe. In order for this to be possible, however, the country must have ready access to adequate supplies of foreign exchange in this period and the authorities must be prepared to use these resources to see the economy through the period until the balance of payments position begins to improve.

3 *Foreign Ownership of Canadian Resources*

In the past few years there has been in Canada a very active discussion concerning foreign ownership.[19] In the course of this analysis we have developed some points which are relevant to an understanding of the forces which have led to the large-scale foreign ownership of Canadian resources and it seems appropriate to discuss this question here.

The current account of the Canadian balance of international payments tends to be passive except when the economy is very depressed and domestic investment is at a low ebb.[20] And, as the economy becomes more prosperous, the size of the passive balance increases. Now, to say that a country has a passive balance of payments on current account is just another way of saying that the value of purchases of goods and services from non-residents (imports) exceeds the value of sales of goods and services to non-residents (exports). In such a case the excess of the value of imports over that of exports can only be met by drawing on reserves or by borrowing abroad. The first alternative is not relevant for a long-continued passive balance and so the passive balance must in practice be financed by borrowing abroad. And the counterpart of borrowing abroad is increasing the claims of non-residents on resources situated in Canada. Moreover, the more prosperous we become the larger becomes the passive current account balance and, as a necessary corollary of this, the more rapidly does foreign ownership increase. This pattern has persisted for at least one hundred years and is simply a reflection of the fact that, except under very depressed conditions, Canada, with its large endowment of natural resources, is a most attractive country in which to invest.[21] Thus the tendency toward the increase in foreign ownership is a reflection of deep-seated and persistent economic forces.

It would appear that the concern about this matter is political rather than economic. It may or may not be desirable on political grounds to slow up or stop the increase in foreign ownership, but it seems clear from our economic analysis that any attempt to make a major change in this matter would run counter to powerful economic forces. The introduction of such a policy would inevitably slow up the rate of growth of the economy (since domestic saving could not in practice be increased enough to replace the reduction in the net foreign capital inflows) and, in this and other ways, it would almost certainly do great and lasting economic damage to both the internal and the external position of the economy.

APPENDICES
A
Econometric Methods

In this appendix we shall consider the problems of statistical and econometric theory which arose in the course of this study and shall give the reasons for adopting the particular techniques used. It is not, of course, proposed to develop the general theorems on which the estimation procedures are based; such material is available in the literature and need not be reproduced here.[1] Our purpose is rather to consider how best to choose, from established statistical and econometric techniques, those which are most appropriate in the context of the present study and to attempt some assessment of the extent to which the techniques employed are adequate to deal with the problems encountered.

The core of the hypothesis developed in Chapter 1 consists of three relationships, each of which can be represented by a behavioural equation:

1 Canada's current account credits depend upon incomes in other countries, on the relative price of Canada's exports, and on the relationship of export prices to domestic costs.

2 The GNE in Canada depends upon the level of exports and of domestic investment.

3 Canada's current account debits depend upon the level of income in Canada and the relative prices (including customs duties) of imports compared with domestic prices in Canada.

It is reasonable, as a first approximation at least, to consider that in each of these equations there is a "one-way direction of causation," i.e., that the causation runs from the variables on the right-hand side of the equation to the dependent variable on the left-hand side. In considering the first equation above, it is not unreasonable to claim that the volume of Canada's exports has but little influence on the explanatory variables in this relationship. Klein, for example, mentions that "International trading relationships pitting a small country's demand or supply against an overwhelming world may also be estimated by the ordinary methods of least squares."[2]

A somewhat similar argument applies for the third equation. Here again, as a first approximation, we can treat the variables on the right-hand side of the equation (domestic income and the price of imports relative to the domestic price level) as exogenous in this context.[3]

Concerning the second equation, somewhat different considerations are relevant. It is technically correct to estimate the relationship by the method of ordinary least squares provided we can assume that the explanatory variables (exports and domestic investment) are not influenced by the magnitude of the variable (GNE) which is treated as dependent. For exports this is a reasonable assumption. The same assumption is often made for domestic investment, and in Chapter 6 we have followed this practice. However, as an additional check we assumed that investment had two constituents. One was taken to be the autonomous element which was regarded as independent of the level of income. The other was treated as being dependent, respectively, on exports and on other constituents of GNE, both in the preceding year. It is of interest that the coefficient relating GNE to exports had nearly the same value in this case as in that in which we treated investment simply as an exogenous variable.

We conclude that it is appropriate (and this is consistent with either of the approaches described in the preceding paragraph) to use ordinary least squares as an estimating technique.[4] However, for reasons which will become evident later in this appendix equations are derived from the absolute first differences of the respective variables rather than from the original values of those variables. For each of the major equations we have also calculated a regression based on the year-to-year percentage changes (percentage first differences) of the respective variables.

If, then, we conclude that the method of ordinary least squares (applied to the first differences of the variables) is an appropriate one to use in this instance, we have still a number of additional problems to consider. The remainder of this appendix will be concerned with the statistical and econometric techniques which have been employed (or with reasons for taking no action) to deal with (1) the trend, (2) multicollinearity, (3) specification of the model, (4) small number of observations, (5) errors or bias in the variables, (6) the aggregation problem, and (7) leads and lags in the relationships among the variables.

1 THE TREND

It is frequently found that economic time series reflect the influence of factors which operate persistently, although usually slowly, over long periods of time and so give rise to long-term trends. The presence of such trends in the data will have a disturbing effect on the results of the statistical analysis and so we must provide some means of dealing with this matter.[5]

Ideally, we should like to include in the regression analysis a quantitative measure of each influence which contributes to the presence of trend, but such a procedure is seldom feasible. For this there are at least three possible reasons. First, the exact causes of the trend may not be known and it is often not possible, in the context of a particular study where the primary focus of interest is on some other matter, to determine precisely what influences have been responsible for the trend in the data. To say that we should not proceed until these matters have been fully explored is often a counsel of perfection which would be an effective barrier to further progress.

Second, the factors which are responsible for the trend may be known but it may not be possible to measure them in such a manner that the results of the measurement can be included in a regression analysis. The causal factors are likely to be such developments as changes in tastes, in technology, or in economic structure. The difficulty of reducing such factors to quantitative terms which could be used in a regression analysis is obvious.

Third, the factors which contribute to the trend may be so numerous that to include each of them explicitly would reduce unduly the number of degrees of freedom. In addition, such a procedure would be very likely to accentuate the problem of multicollinearity. Either of these influences would tend to increase the standard errors of the regression parameters and so could make it impossible to say anything with a reasonable degree of confidence about the influence of any one of the explanatory variables on the behaviour of the dependent variable.

Because of such difficulties it is customary to use time as a substitute variable. Time is not an economic variable, but the influence of these other factors is likely to be cumulative over time and so it is often desirable to use time to represent these other variables which are unknown, unmeasurable, or too numerous to include separately. The coefficient of the time variable is then a measure of the combined effect of these trend factors.

The regression analyses in this study have been computed from the first differences of the various time series. In such cases the constant term in the regression equation provides a measure of the trend.[6] Thus the use of a constant term in the first difference regression equations has the effect both of providing an estimate of the size of the trend factor and, by providing for it separately, of minimizing the danger that the presence of a trend element will distort the values of the other parameters.

2   MULTICOLLINEARITY

The marked tendency toward a similar pattern of behaviour for many economic series is an essential feature of the business cycle, but this tendency toward multicollinearity can be the cause of difficulties in the area of regression analysis. When we are using such series as our explanatory variables it is often impossible to isolate statistically the influence of the individual explanatory variable on the variable whose behaviour we wish to explain; the standard errors of the regression coefficients in such cases are often so large relative to the regression coefficients themselves that the latter are of little value.

The use of the first differences rather than the original data usually has the effect of reducing the multicollinearity among the explanatory variables because *changes* in the values of the explanatory variables are likely to exhibit less multicollinearity than do the original values. This consideration, therefore, provides yet another reason for using the first differences.

3   SPECIFICATION OF THE MODEL

In considering the specification of the model we must recognize that it is feasible, given the nature of the data and the fact that we have no more than twelve observations, to include only a small number of variables in any one equation. We are limited, in practice, in any one equation to two or three explanatory variables and the question is whether we have included a variable which, for our purposes, is less important than some other variable which could have been, but was not, included.

Our purpose is to test the particular hypothesis which was developed in the first chapter of this study and so our choice of variables is restricted (in the first instance, at least) to those mentioned either explicitly or by implication in that hypothesis. Consequently, the variables included in the equations are those suggested by the hypothesis which is being tested. It might, for example, have been possible in some cases to have secured a better "fit" if we had used current income and lagged income as our independent variables rather than current income and relative prices. This alternative formulation would be appropriate if we were primarily concerned with the lag structure of the relationship; but our purpose is rather to test an hypothesis and for this we must use the variables which it suggests before we consider using others. The variables that are included in the equations developed in Chapters 4, 5, and 6 have been chosen on the basis of this criterion and so they can be regarded as appropriate, at least in a general sense, to the purpose for which they were chosen.

4   THE SMALL NUMBER OF OBSERVATIONS

The small number of observations has the effect both of severely limiting the number of explanatory variables which it is feasible to include and of increasing the difficulty of obtaining standard errors of parameters which are small relative to the size of the parameters themselves. Fortunately, it has been possible to secure results which are reasonably satisfactory, in terms of the accepted statistical criteria, for all the central relationships suggested by our hypothesis. And since the tests of significance which were used have all been corrected for the number of degrees of freedom it is possible to say that the difficulties which stem from the small number of observations have been overcome.

It is, however, true in only a restricted sense that these difficulties have been overcome. If there were more observations it would be possible to explore the relationships more fully and, in particular, to investigate the chronological, as well as the analytical, order of events. For the interwar period there is little that can be done about this with the data which are available.[7] The GNE series does not begin until 1926 and by 1940, at the latest, the economy was seriously disrupted by war. The maximum possible length of the interwar period for which data are available is fourteen years (thirteen first differences) and even this number is obtained only by including 1939. We have preferred not to include this latter year in the present study but an argument could be made against this decision.

A difficulty which is more serious than the small number of years is the absence of sufficient quarterly data to permit us to consider quarterly rather than the annual periods for the interwar years. The use of such data, if it were available, would greatly increase the number of degrees of freedom and not only permit a more detailed analysis but, in particular, it would make possible a study of the time relationships in the model. Fortunately, quarterly data are available for the postwar period, beginning with 1947. It is hoped in a later study to use this material both to permit a comparison of the postwar with the interwar period and also to fill in for the later period some of the lacunae in this analysis of the 1926–38 period.

5 ERRORS OF MEASUREMENT

It has thus far been assumed implicitly that all the data have been free from errors of measurement. This is, of course, not true, and it has been shown by Orcutt that random errors of measurement "will bias the income and price elasticities toward zero, whether or not such errors are present in the quantity series."[8] If we assume that the errors of measurement are random, we can conclude, on the basis of Orcutt's analysis, that the true values of the income and price coefficients, although they would be unknown, would tend to be further from zero than the values as determined from our regression calculations.

There are three further points which require some discussion here. These deal, respectively, with the probable cyclical pattern of error in the price and income series, with the probable magnitude of the errors, and with the implications of the fact that our analysis is based on first differences.

It seems probable that in the series used the cyclical pattern of errors of measurement is such as to accentuate the fluctuations in the explanatory variables in both the export and the import equations (Chapters 4 and 5, and Appendices H and I). In the import equation, to consider it first, the explanatory variables are changes in per capita income in Canada (at 1935–9 prices) and changes in the ratio of the price of imports (including the tariff) to the appropriate index of domestic prices in Canada. When incomes fall it is probable that the official statistics will tend to exaggerate the decline because it seems likely that in such circumstances a rather larger proportion of income will escape the net of the national income statistician since, for example, people will tend to perform for themselves services for which they had formerly paid others and some transactions which were formerly conducted on a cash basis will now be on a barter basis.

A similar argument applies in connection with price declines in a period of declining economic activity and falling prices. Special sales and other concessions to buyers tend to be more important in such periods and are unlikely to be fully reflected in official price statistics. The opposite effects would be expected in periods of expanding economic activity and rising prices.

These influences seem unlikely to be so great for imports, because the transactions are, in general, subject to closer inspection with a corresponding increase in the quality of the statistics. In addition the buyers and sellers are in less intimate contact so that the likelihood of special concessions which are not reflected in the statistics is reduced. The result of any of these systematic cyclical effects which may be reflected in the import series is further to bias downward the income and price coefficients.

For the export case a similar argument applies and it would be both tedious and unnecessary to develop it fully here because it parallels that which we have just presented for imports. Our conclusion regarding the coefficients in both the export and the import equations is that the random errors of measurement will bias them toward zero and that this bias will be re-enforced by the systematic cyclical errors.

The situation for the domestic income equation (Chapter 6) is somewhat different. The explanatory variables in this instance are per capita exports and per capita domestic investment (both at 1935–9 prices) while the dependent variable is per capita GNE at 1935–9 prices. In this equation, applying the argument given immediately above, the dependent variable would seem likely to have more systematic cyclical error in it than has the export variable and the *systematic* bias for the coefficient of the export variable would seem likely, on balance, to be upward.

It is more difficult to assess the relative magnitude of any systematic cyclical bias in the domestic determinants of income compared with the bias in the income variable; it is, therefore, assumed that this coefficient has the downward bias which would result from the presence of random errors only.

We turn now from considering the errors in the data to dealing with the measures which were taken to minimize the errors and their effects. Before this is done, however, it may be mentioned that the original data are considered, with only a few exceptions, to be of good quality and so the bias introduced from this source is relatively small. Moreover, a good deal of care has been taken in processing the data so that the effects of such errors on the values of the parameters have been kept to a minimum. The procedures involved are described more fully in the relevant appendices.

The use of first differences would also seem to have the incidental effect of reducing bias. An error which appears consistently throughout a series would be minimized by taking the first differences since, for example, a constant error would not affect the absolute magnitude of the period-to-period changes.[9] The elimination of trend effects would also reduce the effect of errors which tended to vary cumulatively with the passage of time since the systematic part of such errors would be reflected in the trend term, i.e., the constant term in the first difference regression equation.

In conclusion, then, it is felt that nearly all of the data used are of good quality and that the techniques used have been such as to minimize the effects on the parameters of errors of measurement. Nevertheless, it is probable that both random and systematic errors are present in the data and the best that can be said is that these errors are thought to be somewhere near a minimum for aggregative data of this type. It seems reasonable to conclude also that the presence of such errors is likely to have the effect of biasing the estimates of the values of the parameters toward zero.

6   AGGREGATION

The relationships with which we are concerned extend over many commodities and many individuals and so we are confronted with the problem of aggregation. The aggregate relationships are simply derived from the individual relationships provided the latter are "purely linear with constant coefficients for all units in the society or if all incomes (or prices) change in the same proportion."[10]

It is not possible, on the basis of strictly *a priori* considerations, to reach any firm conclusion as to the existence of either of these conditions. We may safely assume that neither is valid in any absolute sense, but experience drawn from other similar investigations suggests that the assumption involved here may be, and in at least some cases is, a sufficiently good approximation to the truth to make it useful for practical purposes of estimation. If one or the other (or both) of the conditions mentioned above were known to be satisfied by the data, special measures to deal with this aggregation problem would not be required.

Since we cannot confidently assume the validity of either of these two conditions, it is desirable to undertake some measure of disaggregation. The results are presented in Appendices F and G, which deal, respectively, with Canada's exports to the United States and with the disaggregation of total current account debits into twelve groups. Appendix E, which considers exports of non-monetary gold, may also be regarded as a measure of disaggregation.

The second reason for introducing some disaggregation is methodological in nature and is considered by the writer to be of greater importance in the present context. In fitting the regressions, it is desirable to experiment with a number of different approaches in order to decide upon the one or two which are most satisfactory in meeting the relevant tests as to economic plausibility and statistical significance. But it may be that the method which gives the "best" results in a particular instance does so merely because of the chance patterns of stochastic effects in that instance and it may have no inherent superiority over other methods which, for the available set of data, give less satisfactory results.

One way to introduce a further test is to apply the same method to the individual components of the data in disaggregated form. If it gives acceptable results in these cases as well as in the case where aggregates are used our confidence in the method is multiplied.

7 LEADS AND LAGS

It is reasonable to expect that there will be differences in the timing of the changes in the different variables. This implies that it would be desirable to make some provision for leads and lags in our equations. In fact this has not been done, except in one or two very minor instances, and this omission requires some explanation.

There are four reasons for this omission. First, the regression calculations are based on the first differences of time series which have been deflated for both population and price changes, i.e., the data have already been subject to a good deal of processing. If, in addition to these adjustments, we were to introduce provision for leads and lags, the connection with the original data would be made both more complex and more tenuous.

Second, we deal with annual data and it is improbable that the principal leads and lags are more than a small fraction of a year. The omission of provision for leads and lags is less important when we use annual data than it would be if the figures applied to shorter intervals of time.

Third, the introduction of leads and lags into the equations would further reduce the already small number of degrees of freedom and, depending upon the method used, could also substantially increase the degree of multicollinearity among the explanatory variables.[11]

Finally, the introduction of leads and lags in such cases may have, and in the writer's experience usually has, the effect of improving the correlation but makes little differenee to the values of the regression coefficients. In this study the correlation coefficients arc, almost without exception, very high. It has seemed that any improvement here would probably not be sufficient to compensate for the difficulties and problems which would arise if leads and lags were introduced into the equations.

There would be a much stronger case for introducing leads and lags if we had quarterly data for the 1926–38 period as we have for the postwar period, beginning in 1947. Both the shorter time intervals and the greater number of degrees of freedom would provide arguments in favour of introducing provision for leads and lags. For the interwar period it has seemed preferable not to make special provision for this factor.

B
Canadian and World Trade in Goods and Services

This appendix explains the derivation of the figures for world trade in goods and services in each of the years 1928, 1932, 1935, and 1938. We consider first the current dollar figures which are used in Table IV and then the deflation of these figures to remove from them the effects of price changes.

The principal source used was *The Network of World Trade*.[1] The totals shown in this publication include a very high proportion of the world's total commodity trade in 1928, 1935, and 1938. The figures for all countries are expressed in United States gold dollars at the parity rate established in 1934 and, in addition, the 1928 figures are given on the basis of the then current value of the dollar. Figures are not given for 1932 but the data for that year are available from *Review of World Trade, 1938*.[2]

The export figures given in these two publications do not include transport costs beyond the borders of the exporting country, but the import figures do include such costs up to the frontier of the importing country.[3] The difference between the import and the export figures can be used as a measure of the cost of transport internationally and, in fact, the figures have been checked by those who prepared them to ensure that this difference is a reasonable measure of transport costs between countries.[4] The value of trade in gold and silver is given in Annex II of *The Network of World Trade*. Data representing a high proportion of the international receipts from interest and dividends, tourist services, and emigrants' remittances are also available.[5] The sum of these items (all expressed in current United States dollars) gives the total for world exports of goods and services as shown in Table IV.

We wish also to have a measure of total world current account credits valued at constant prices and for this we require price indexes with which to deflate the figures in Table IV. For commodity trade (excluding gold and silver) we can use the price index figures from *The Network of World Trade* and from *Review of World Trade, 1938*. For freight and shipping we constructed a composite price index from the index numbers of ocean freight rates for the major countries involved in this aspect of world trade.[6] The current values of gold and silver were adjusted to obtain their respective values in each year at constant prices.

The deflation of the current dollar values for tourist and travel, interest and dividends, and emigrants' remittances presented a more difficult problem for which we were not able to find an ideal solution. The procedure adopted was to calculate a composite index of the cost of living from the separate indexes for the major countries and this index was then used to deflate the three balance of payments items mentioned above. This deflation procedure gives only a rough approximation to the values of these items at constant prices but it is felt that the deflated figures reflect the general trends without serious distortion. These items in total averaged only 10 per cent of the figure for all current account credits in Table IV (and they did not exceed 12 per cent in any of the four years). Consequently, any error which may be introduced by the deflation procedure used for these items will be small in relation both to world current account credits and to changes in them. We require merely a general measure of Canada's trade in relation to that of the rest of the world and the method we have used here gives results which are adequate for our purposes.

C
The Measurement of Unemployment in Canada, 1926

This appendix has a double purpose. It provides a more detailed explanation than was given in Chapter 3 of the method used to make the required estimates of a full employment income and it presents the statistical data from which these estimates were derived.

The general procedure, as sketched in Chapter 3, was to select a prosperous year near the beginning of the period and another near the end of the period. For each of these years an estimate was made of what a full employment income would have been and from these two bench-marks the comparable figures for the other years of the period were calculated.

We begin by looking for a year in the early part of the period in which full employment, or a condition close to full employment, was realized. Any one of the three years 1927, 1928, or 1929 would satisfy this requirement. We shall choose 1929 because it is closest to the census year 1931 and the nearer to the census year the more reliable the figures are likely to be; this is a more important consideration in the early part of the period when the data are somewhat less reliable than for later years. In addition, 1929 was the last year of prosperity before the depression of the 1930s and so it provides a better basis for interpolation into this period than would an earlier year.

The problem is to estimate what a full employment GNE, valued at 1935–9 prices, would have been in 1929 for the non-agricultural sectors of the economy. Our procedure involves three steps. First, we estimate the average number of unemployed in 1929 after allowing for any disguised unemployment there may have been in that year. Second, we make an estimate of the percentage of the non-agricultural labour force which would have been unemployed in 1929 if there had been full employment. Third, we use this information to make an estimate of the full employment GNE for 1929. Throughout this appendix the terms *full employment income* and *full employment* GNE are used to mean the non-agricultural full employment GNE valued in terms of 1935–9 prices. We shall not, however, be concerned so much with any single estimate of the full employment income as with assessing the limits within which we can feel confident the required figure would lie.

The first step is to estimate the average number of unemployed workers in 1929, including in this figure an allowance for any disguised unemployment there may have been. To do this we begin with the total labour force and deduct from this figure the number of workers that would have been required in agriculture in 1929. This gives us the number of workers that would have been available, under conditions of full employment, to the non-agricultural sectors. From this figure for the total non-agricultural labour force we subtract average employment in the non-agricultural sectors. This is our best estimate of average unemployment for 1929. However, we shall also derive upper and lower limits between which we can have a high degree of confidence the "correct" figure (if it could be known) would be found.

The results of such calculations for 1929 are summarized in Table xx. The method of arriving at these figures is explained below.

TABLE XX
DISTRIBUTION OF THE LABOUR FORCE, 1929

	Position at 1 June 1929	1929 average unemployment		
		Most probable	Upper estimate	Lower estimate
		(thousands of persons)		
Total civilian labour force	3,964	3,944	3,964	3,924
Armed services	5	5	5	5
Total labour force	3,969	3,949	3,969	3,929
Required in agriculture at full employment	1,307	1,300	1,275	1,325
Non-agricultural labour force	2,662	2,649	2,694	2,604
Actual non-agricultural employment	2,546	2,480	2,460	2,500
Unemployed	116	169	234	104
Acceptable unemployment*		93	68	130
Unemployed in excess of acceptable unemployment		76	166	−26
Estimated unemployment as percentage of the non-agricultural labour force	4·4%	6·4%	8·7%	4·0%

*For acceptable unemployment the "most probable" figure is taken to be 3·5 per cent of the non-agricultural labour force; the corresponding minimum figure is 2·5 per cent and the maximum figure is 5·0 per cent.

Sources: Dominion Bureau of Statistics, *National Accounts, Income and Expenditure*, 1926 to 1956, Appendix, Table II, 100; Bank of Canada, *Statistical Summary, 1961 Supplement*, 130–3; Dominion Bureau of Statistics, *Canadian Labour Force Estimates 1931–1945*, Reference Paper 23, revised (Ottawa 1957), 20; Dominion Bureau of Statistics, *Historical Monthly Statistics* (Ottawa 1964), 35–9; W. C. Hood and A. Scott, *Output Labour and Capital in the Canadian Economy* (Ottawa 1957), 196.

The first column of the table shows the distribution of the labour force, as given in the official sources, at 1 June 1929. Consideration of the economic circumstances which had prevailed for some time prior to this date suggests that there would be no more disguised unemployment represented in these data than one would find under favourable economic conditions and so the official figures are left unchanged for this date.

We are interested, however, in the average labour force distribution for the year rather than in the figures for any one date and so the figures in the first column of the table must be adjusted accordingly. This has been done in the last three columns of Table xx.

The upper estimate of the average number unemployed in 1929 was reached by taking an upper estimate of the total labour force figure together with a lower estimate of the average number employed in both the agricultural and the non-agricultural sectors. The converse procedure was adopted to secure the lower estimate of unemployment. From Table xx it is seen that the estimates of unemployment vary from an upper figure of 8·7 per cent to a lower figure of 4·0 per cent; the "most probable" figure is 6·4 per cent of the non-agricultural labour force.

We have arrived at estimates of the amount of unemployment in Canada in 1929 as a percentage of the non-agricultural labour force. This is the first step in our procedure for estimating what a full employment income would have been. The second step is to assess the limits within which this percentage would be expected to lie under conditions of full employment.

There were no years in the period 1926–38, apart from the late 1920s, when full employment was reached or even closely approached and so we shall turn to the postwar period when there were years of prosperity and for which, an important consideration from our point of view, the statistics of unemployment are much more reliable.

Our purpose is to determine the range within which total unemployment, expressed as a percentage of the non-agricultural labour force, would have fallen under conditions of full employment. This range we shall designate as that of "acceptable unemployment." When we have arrived at the appropriate range for acceptable unemployment in the first decade after World War II we shall return to consider the 1929 experience in the light of the conclusions reached for the postwar period. This analysis will be supplemented by consideration of the behaviour of employment and wage rates in the period 1928–30.

Table XXI shows unemployment as a percentage of the non-agricultural labour force in each of the years 1947–55 inclusive.

In no year of this generally prosperous period did average unemployment fall below 2·4 per cent of the non-agricultural labour force. In the three years of the period (1947, 1948, and 1951) when inflationary pressure was greatest and both prices and wage rates

TABLE XXI
UNEMPLOYMENT IN THE POSTWAR PERIOD 1947–55

Year	Labour Force* (thousands)	Unemployment (thousands)	Unemployment %
1947†	3,855	98	2·5
1948	3,928	102	2·6
1949	4,120	144	3·5
1950	4,190	166	4·0
1951	4,352	106	2·4
1952	4,522	129	2·9
1953	4,630	137	3·0
1954	4,667	232	5·0
1955	4,858	230	4·7

*The labour force figures include the armed services but exclude agriculture. Both labour force and unemployment figures are averages for the respective years.
†The first postwar year, 1946, is not useful for our purposes because demobilization of the armed services was in progress for much of the year. The unemployment figure for that year was 4·1 per cent.

Sources: See sources cited for Table xx.

were rising rapidly, unemployment was 2·5, 2·6, and 2·4 per cent, respectively. This indicates clearly that acceptable unemployment would be somewhat greater than 2·5 per cent. We shall be safe in setting this figure as the lower limit of the range for acceptable unemployment in the first postwar decade.

The highest percentages of unemployment were reached in 1954 and 1955 when the figures were 5·0 and 4·7 per cent, respectively. Since these figures relate to years which are generally regarded as being years of something less than full employment, we can safely say that the upper limit for acceptable unemployment in this period would not have exceeded 5 per cent on the average for the year.[1]

We have fixed the upper and lower limits for acceptable unemployment during the first postwar decade and must now fix the single figure which seems most appropriate. Since we are concerned primarily with the range within which the figure would fall rather than with any one value, this figure is less important than those which fix the upper and lower limits. But it is convenient, if nothing more, to have one single figure which seems best.

One way of arriving at such a single figure is simply to take the average of the upper and lower estimates which we have already established; this average is 3¾ per cent of the non-agricultural labour force.

A second, and rather more satisfactory method is to look again at the postwar period. Of the nine years 1947 to 1955 inclusive, we have seen that three were clearly years of inflation and in two others economic conditions seem to have fallen somewhat short of full employment. This leaves four years (1949, 1950, 1952, and 1953) which come somewhere in between, and a case could be made for any one of these as a year of full employment.[2] The average of the four has the advantage of reflecting the experience of several years. We can take this average as another estimate of the best single figure; it is 3·4 per cent.

A third alternative is to adopt the figure used in some other study. The Royal Commission on Canada's Economic Prospects, deriving its estimate from the period 1950–5, uses 3 per cent of the total labour force.[3] This is equivalent, for the period in question, to 3·6 per cent of the non-agricultural labour force. Finally, the Bank of Canada in its *Annual Report* for 1950 takes 1949 as a year of full employment.[4] In that year unemployment averaged 3·5 per cent of the non-agricultural labour force.

These estimates are all clustered in a narrow range around a figure of approximately 3·5 per cent. We shall adopt this figure as the best single estimate of acceptable unemployment in the decade immediately following World War II.

We have considered, up to this point, only the postwar period and only the test which is based on percentage unemployment. Before we can reach any final conclusion we must consider unemployment in the earlier period and it will also be desirable to apply an additional test for the existence of full employment in 1929.

We know, without examining them in detail, that 1927 and 1928 were prosperous years. In fact, unemployment in 1929 was greater than it was in either of these two earlier years, but examination of the statistics for 1927 and 1928 does not indicate the presence of overfull employment or inflation. If we take the official (June 1st) figure for unemployment in each of these years and adjust it to an annual average basis as we did in 1929, the figure for each year lies between 3 and 4 per cent of the non-agricultural labour force. The statistical data for these early years have a greater relative margin of error than have the postwar figures but, taken at their face value and in conjunction with the other evidence, they suggest that acceptable unemployment in the late 1920s was in the same range as we have found to apply in the years just after World War II. And, if this is true, it follows that 1929 probably fell slightly short of being a year of full employment.

We need to supplement the tests based on employment data and so shall also consider the behaviour of wage rates compared with that of average numbers employed in 1929. On general theoretical grounds we would expect that, as an economy expanded towards full employment, it would become more and more difficult to increase the number employed. In these circumstances it would be in wage rates, rather than in numbers employed, that the more marked increases would be expected.

The application of this test also leads to the conclusion that 1929 was a year of something less than full employment. The annual average index of employment in 1929 exceeded that for 1928 by 6 per cent; the excess of the peak month of 1929 over the peak month of 1928 was also 6 per cent.[5] The increase in average wage rates from 1928 to 1929 was less than 2 per cent. The general index of wage rates increased slightly in 1930 but, even if we include 1930 in order to allow for a substantial lag, it is found that over the period 1928 to 1930, the index of wage rates rose by less than $2\frac{1}{2}$ per cent.

It appears, on the basis of all the evidence we have considered, that 1929 probably fell somewhat short of being a year of full employment. Since it would also be a year of less than full employment in terms of the figures for acceptable unemployment in the postwar years, we conclude that the figures derived for this measure for the postwar years would apply also to 1929.

We are now in a position to compare average estimated unemployment in 1929 with what it would have been under conditions of full employment. Our "most probable" figure for average unemployment is 169 thousand and our best estimate of acceptable unemployment is 3.5 per cent; in 1929 this would be 93 thousand. Thus our best estimate is that in 1929 actual average employment fell short of the full employment level by 76 thousand.

We are more interested, however, in the upper and lower limits between which the true value can be expected to lie than in any single figure. In order to derive the upper limit of this range we pair up the maximum estimate of actual unemployment with the minimum figure for acceptable unemployment; and by a converse procedure we arrive at the lower limit of this range. The calculations are shown in the last two columns of Table xx; they indicate that in 1929 average unemployment may have exceeded acceptable unemployment by an estimated maximum of 166 thousand on the one extreme or, on the other, that it was 26 less than it would have been under conditions of full employment, but not inflation, in 1929.

What would have been the quantitative effect on the 1929 GNE of increasing non-agricultural employment by 76 or 166 thousand on the one hand or of reducing it by 26 thousand on the other? Some light is thrown on this matter by the data in Table xxii and especially by the last column of that table.

Even after allowing for secular growth in productivity at a plausible rate, these figures give no indication of diminishing returns to labour on a man-year basis as employment increased. We shall assume that, within the relevant range, there were constant returns to labour equal to the average GNE per person employed in the non-agricultural sectors.[6] This average for 1929 was $2,002 at 1935–9 prices.

In order to obtain our estimates of a full employment income in 1929 we need only take the actual figure for the non-agricultural GNE and add (subtract) the total contribution to GNE of the increase (decrease) in the number of workers. This calculation gives us, as Table xxiv shows, a "most probable" GNE of $5,117 million; the upper figure is $5,299 million and the lower figure is $4,913 million.

These upper and lower estimates have been arrived at by a pairing of opposite extreme assumptions in each case. It is most improbable that all of these assumptions would be realized and, therefore, the range for our full employment figure is almost certainly wider than it needs to be. In this connection it is relevant to mention that our lower estimate for a full employment GNE assumes that 1929 was a year of more than full employment although our analysis has led to the conclusion that there was something less than full employment in that year. But the range calculated above is sufficiently narrow for our purposes and so, in order to have a high degree of confidence that the range we specify contains within it the "correct" figure, we shall use the range calculated above ($4,913 to $5,299 million) without attempting to narrow it further.

Estimates have been made of what a full employment GNE would have been for a year which comes near the beginning of the period and it is now necessary to make a similar

TABLE XXII
EMPLOYMENT AND GROSS NATIONAL EXPENDITURE IN THE NON-AGRICULTURAL SECTORS

Year	GNE (at 1935–9 prices)	Net income in agriculture (millions)	Index of farm living costs	Agri-cultural income at 1935–9 prices (millions)	Non-ag. GNE at 1935–9 prices* (millions)	Non-ag. employ-ment† (thousands)	GNE per capita (at 1935–9 prices)
1926	$4,430	$609	121·1	$503	$3,927	2,244	$1,750
1927	4,836	600	119·8	501	4,335	2,353	1,842
1928	5,285	636	118·5	537	4,748	2,449	1,939
1929	5,299	392	117·3	334	4,965	2,480	2,002
1930	5,075	343	113·7	302	4,773	2,390	1,997
1931	4,425	94	103·9	90	4,335	2,432	1,782
1932	3,975	104	97·8	106	3,869	2,198	1,760
1933	3,719	66	95·8	69	3,650	2,124	1,718
1934	4,168	167	97·9	171	3,997	2,420	1,652
1935	4,490	218	97·9	223	4,267	2,529	1,687
1936	4,691	199	98·3	202	4,489	2,626	1,709
1937	5,158	280	102·9	272	4,886	2,777	1,759
1938	5,188	353	101·9	346	4,842	2,711	1,786
1939	5,577	362	99·5	364	5,191	2,770	1,874
1940	6,381	483	108·5	445	5,763	2,927	1,969
1941	7,302	463	114·0	406	6,553	3,045	2,152

*Excludes military pay and allowances in excess of the estimated peacetime level in 1939, 1940, and 1941. The amounts excluded are $22, $173, and $343 million, respectively.
†Excludes members of the armed forces in excess of the estimated peacetime level in 1939, 1940, and 1941. The numbers excluded are 19, 155, and 305 thousand, respectively.

Sources: *National Accounts*, 32, 36, 100; *Prices and Price Indexes*, 1949–52, 93.

estimate for a year that comes near the end of the period. In order to make the most satisfactory estimate possible it is desirable to make it for a year in which conditions approaching full employment were experienced.

Here a difficulty arises since depression persisted throughout the 1930s. Even in 1937, the most prosperous peacetime year of the later 1930s, unemployment, excluding a substantial amount of disguised unemployment, was 13 per cent of the non-agricultural labour force.[7] A year which fell so far short of being one of full employment is not a good one for our present purpose.

In the early war years, shortly after the period covered by this study, full employment appears to have been reached but only under wartime conditions, which might affect the estimate. Moreover, a special difficulty arises because as early as 1941, for example, the average number in the armed services was 315 thousand. Apart from this difficulty, 1941 would appear to be the most satisfactory year for the present purpose, especially when it is recalled that the most significant wartime controls were not put into effect until later.[8] It is, therefore, proposed to estimate what a full employment income would have been in 1941 under peacetime conditions. Figures for the years between 1929 and 1941 will be arrived at by interpolation, and the series will be extrapolated to cover the years 1926 to 1928.

In making the estimate of a full employment national income for 1941 we must deal with the complication that there were 315 thousand in the armed services. We shall assume that, under peacetime conditions, there would have been only 10 thousand in the armed services and that the remaining 305 thousand would have been in the civilian labour force. In order to be consistent with this approach we must deduct the amount of military pay

TABLE XXIII
DISTRIBUTION OF THE LABOUR FORCE, 1941 (in thousands of persons)

		Annual average		
	Position at 1 June 1941	Most probable	Upper estimate of unemployment	Lower estimate of unemployment
Total civilian labour force	4,466	4,444	4,466	4,422
Armed services		315	315	315
Total labour force		4,759	4,781	4,737
Required in agriculture at full employment	1,224	1,200	1,175	1,225
Non-agricultural labour force		3,559	3,606	3,512
Non-agricultural civilian employment plus requirement for peacetime armed forces		3,045	3,015	3,075
Unemployed plus armed services in excess of peacetime requirement		514	591	437
Acceptable unemployment		125	90	176
Deficiency of non-agricultural civilian employment below peacetime full employment		389	501	261

Sources: See Table xx.

and allowances (at 1935–9 prices) estimated to have been received by these 305 thousand persons. We then treat the 305 thousand as part of the regular civilian labour force and proceed to estimate the full employment peacetime GNE accordingly.

Table XXIII shows the details for the estimated distribution of the labour force in 1941. The first column shows the position on 1 June 1941 as reported in the official statistics and, since this was a decennial census date, there is probably a minimum margin of error in these figures. The figures in the other three columns were calculated in a manner analogous to that for 1929. The last line of this table shows that, after providing for the armed services on a peacetime basis and allowing for acceptable unemployment, the number of employed civilians in 1941 averaged from 261 thousand to 501 thousand less than the estimated figure if there had been full employment under peacetime conditions; the "most probable" figure is 389 thousand.

Again, as we did for 1929, we must estimate by how much the GNE would be increased if these additional numbers of workers were employed. We shall assume in this case, as we did for 1929, that the marginal product of each additional worker would be the same as the average product of those actually employed.

When we compute the full employment GNE from these figures we find that the estimates range from an upper figure of $7,640 million to a lower figure of $7,109 million; the best single estimate is found to be $7,390 million.

For each of the other years of the period, the per capita full employment GNE for the peacetime non-agricultural labour force was derived from the estimates for 1929 and 1941.[9] The per capita figure obtained in this manner for each year was then applied to the estimated number in the relevant labour force to secure the required full employment income figures for each year.

Finally, the required measures of unemployment are obtained as the differences between the respective measures of full employment GNE and realized GNE in each year. The statistics are shown in Table XXIV.

TABLE XXIV
DEFICIENCY OF NON-AGRICULTURAL GNE BELOW FULL EMPLOYMENT LEVEL, 1926-41

Year	Full employment GNE			Realized non-agricultural GNE	Deficiency of actual below full employment GNE		
	Most probable	upper	lower		Most probable	upper	lower
	(all figures in millions of 1935-9 dollars)						
1926	$4,046	$4,160	$3,918	$3,927	$ 119	$ 233	$ −9
1927	4,386	4,513	4,240	4,335	51	178	−95
1928	4,778	4,908	4,620	4,748	30	160	−128
1929	5,117	5,299	4,913	4,965	152	334	−52
1930	5,353	5,540	5,143	4,773	580	767	370
1931	5,574	5,771	5,359	4,162	1,412	1,609	1,197
1932	5,743	5,946	5,520	3,869	1,874	2,077	1,651
1933	5,918	6,128	5,695	3,650	2,268	2,478	2,045
1934	6,114	6,311	5,862	3,997	2,117	2,314	1,865
1935	6,274	6,499	6,038	4,267	2,007	2,232	1,771
1936	6,461	6,691	6,218	4,489	1,972	2,202	1,729
1937	6,636	6,872	6,379	4,886	1,750	1,986	1,493
1938	6,825	7,064	6,566	4,842	1,983	2,222	1,724
1939	7,050	7,293	6,785	5,191	1,859	2,102	1,594
1940	7,305	7,556	7,028	5,763	1,542	1,793	1,265
1941	7,390	7,640	7,109	6,553	837	1,087	556

D
Exports of Grains and Farinaceous Products

The figures for Canada's current account credits used in Chapter 4 do not include exports of grains and farinaceous products. It is the purpose of this appendix to explain why, in principle, these items should be excluded from the figures used there and to present the relevant empirical evidence for this decision.[1]

In most business enterprises it is true that, if the quantity of factors employed is changed, the resulting change in product can be predicted within narrow limits, except under very unusual circumstances. This is not at all true in the case of the production of vegetable products because of the overwhelming importance to the total yield of crop conditions between the time the crop is planted and the time it has been safely harvested.

Wheat was Canada's most important vegetable product during our period, and the unpredictability of output is illustrated for it in Table xxv.

It will be observed that the number of acres planted to wheat in 1928 was not very different from that planted in 1937, but the crop in the former year was more than three times as large as that in the latter year. To put the same point in another way, we note that the average yield per acre varied from 7·0 bushels to 23·5 bushels. When the crop is planted in the spring, there is no way of knowing whether the yield will be somewhere near the 7

TABLE XXV
WHEAT YIELD PER ACRE 1926–38

Year	Seeded acreage (millions)	Total yield (millions of bushels)	Average yield
1926	22·90	407·1	17·8
1927	22·46	479·7	21·4
1928	24·12	566·7	23·5
1929	25·16	302·2	12·0
1930	24·90	420·7	16·9
1931	26·36	321·3	12·2
1932	27·18	443·1	16·3
1933	25·99	281·9	10·9
1934	23·99	275·8	11·5
1935	24·12	281·9	11·7
1936	25·61	219·2	8·6
1937	25·57	180·2	7·0
1938	25·93	360·0	13·9

Source: Dominion Bureau of Statistics, *Canadian Statistical Review, 1959 Supplement,* 103, 104.

bushel per acre level, the 20 bushel level, or somewhere in between. Moreover, there is variation in the average quality of the crop and this factor can have a major influence on the monetary return from its sale.

For other vegetable products, the fluctuations in yield were less extreme but they were still substantial.[2] However, exports of wheat and wheat flour accounted for between 85 and 90 per cent of the value of total exports of grains and farinaceous products (the other major exports in this group were barley and oats) and so the following treatment is confined to wheat (in which we include the wheat equivalent of wheat flour).

TABLE XXVI
WHEAT – TOTAL SUPPLY AND TOTAL
EXPORTS (all figures in millions of bushels)

Crop year	Total supply	Total exports of wheat and wheat flour
1926–7	447·7	292·9
1927–8	535·8	333·0
1928–9	659·2	407·6
1929–30	430·8	186·3
1930–1	547·5	258·7
1931–2	460·1	207·0
1932–3	579·2	264·3
1933–4	500·0	194·8
1934–5	479·6	165·8
1935–6	496·1	254·4
1936–7	347·0	209·8
1937–8	223·4	95·6
1938–9	386·4	160·0

Source: Dominion Bureau of Statistics, *Canadian Statistical Review, 1959 Supplement,* 108.

Our hypothesis is that wheat exports will depend upon the total supply available. This supply will come partly from current production, partly from the carryover from the previous period, and (a negligible factor) partly from imports. We would expect exports to vary directly with total supply. The figures to test this hypothesis for the crop years 1926–7 to 1938–9 are shown in Table xxvi.

It will be noted that, for each of the crop years shown in the table, exports changed in the same direction as did total supply. The coefficient of simple correlation is $+0.75$, which is significant at the 0.01 level.[3]

We may also compare wheat exports with the level of income in other countries. In this case we find that the two variables changed in the same direction in only four years. The coefficient of simple correlation between these two series is -0.06.

From this analysis we conclude that wheat exports depend primarily upon the supply available (from the carryover plus the current crop) and that the level of income in other countries has little influence. Because wheat and wheat flour exports are such a large proportion of total exports of all grain and farinaceous products and because a similar situation would be expected to apply to the other items in this group, we conclude that we should exclude all exports of grains and farinaceous products from the export figure used in Chapter 4 and this has been done.

We must also examine the possibility that variations in crop yields (and so in grain exports) may have had indirect effects on other exports. This could occur in two ways. First, a large crop might require that resources be diverted from other uses, and, specifically, from the production of other goods for export, to the production and marketing of grain. Second, changes in agricultural production might influence the total of other exports indirectly through their effect on total domestic spending.

The first of these two possibilities would require consideration only if there were not sufficient unemployed resources available to provide the additional factors of production required to handle the large crop. In fact, as we have seen in Chapter 3, during the period after 1929, there were unemployed resources both in agriculture and in other economic sectors in every year of our period. In 1929 the grain crop was substantially smaller than usual and no perceptible diversion of resources from other occupations would be required to deal with the poor crops of that year.[4] We have not examined in detail the years of our period prior to 1929 but in such analyses as we have made there has been no indication of overfull employment.

It is clear that, for the period as a whole, non-agricultural industries were not deprived of resources they wished to employ because the resources were required in agriculture; indeed, the evidence of Chapter 3 shows that, for much of this period, there was disguised unemployment in agriculture which was brought about by the large-scale and persisting unemployment in other sectors of the economy.

More generally, however, the effect of a large crop is to increase activity in the sectors of the economy which are concerned with harvesting, storing, and transporting the crop, and few, if any, resources need to be transferred from other sectors. The transportation and storage facilities are designed to handle a large crop and such a crop merely means that these facilities are more fully utilized.

In the agricultural sector itself, the effect of a large crop is chiefly to increase activity during the harvesting season. Grain is produced principally in the prairie provinces where the harvesting season comes just after the end of the harvesting season on the farms of eastern Canada. This means that some of those who have been employed in harvesting the grain crop in the East, and who would otherwise be in disguised or partial unemployment, can move to the West to work on the harvest there. This movement was greatly facilitated by the familiar "harvest excursions" which permitted workers to travel from the East to help in the western harvest and return for a very moderate fare. The effect of a large crop is, therefore, to increase mobility and reduce disguised unemployment in the agricultural sector with a negligible diversion of productive resources from other sectors of the economy. And, conversely, a small crop is likely to mean less mobility and more under-employment in the agricultural producing and marketing sectors of the economy. In neither case is there likely to be any perceptible effect on exports of other products.

The second way in which changes in agricultural production might be thought to affect other exports would be through its effect on total domestic spending. If we assume, as seems reasonable, that the world demand for Canadian grain products is elastic, then a larger crop will mean larger farm income and so farmers are likely to buy more of both consumer and investment goods.[5] This, in turn, may leave a smaller quantity available for export. Again, this will happen only if there is full employment since otherwise the in-creased demand of the farmers can be met by using resources that would have been unemployed.[6]

It might be thought that production and exports of animal products would also vary significantly with climatic conditions. On the one hand, weather conditions might influence the production of meats and milk (the principal animal products) directly and, on the other hand, changes in grain production would influence the availability of feed grain for live-stock. In fact, however, examination of the statistics reveals that the production both of meats and of milk showed a tendency to fluctuate in sympathy with general economic conditions and neither seems to have been greatly affected in the aggregate by variations from year to year in weather conditions.[7] It will therefore not be necessary to exclude these products from exports and so we shall test our hypothesis concerning exports for all goods and services except grains and farinaceous products.

E
Exports of Non-Monetary Gold

The figures for exports of non-monetary gold are included in those used for total current account credits in Chapter 4 and, in a formal sense at least, it is correct to do this. But the price of gold rose sharply in the years 1930 to 1934 when the general trend of prices, at least until 1932 or 1933, was downward. The value of non-monetary gold exports increased from 2 per cent of total current account credits in the late 1920s to an average of 10 per cent in the second half of the 1930s. In these circumstances it is possible that including gold exports will have the effect of distorting the aggregate export relationship. In this appendix we shall give special consideration to non-monetary gold exports and their effect on the aggregate export equation.

A regression analysis using the value of gold exports as the dependent variable with the supply factor and time as independent variables gave a correlation coefficient of 0·98 and also revealed that almost all of the changes in the value of exports of non-monetary gold in this period could be explained by the trend term in the equation. The coefficient of the supply factor was very small and had a negative sign instead of the positive sign which theoretical considerations would lead us to expect. The important fact revealed by the regression analysis was that the value of non-monetary gold exports (gold being valued throughout at its average 1935–9 price in Canadian dollars) remained very close to its linear trend value throughout the 1926–38 period.

The explanation of the behaviour of gold exports would seem to lie in the particular sequence of developments which influenced gold production in these years. The moderate and irregular expansion of gold exports in the late 1920s was followed by depression and the depreciation of the Canadian dollar relative to the United States dollar in 1930, 1931, and 1932. The increase in the United States dollar price of gold in 1933 and 1934 provided a further stimulus to gold production which was especially effective because other prices were low and unemployment was high in other industries. The result of this series of developments, together with the time required for the gold-mining industry to respond to them, was to cause gold production and exports (nearly all newly-mined gold was exported) to vary but little from its trend value and so it is not possible to show statistically the influence of other factors apart from the trend.

It is possible, therefore, to include gold in the aggregate export equation without distorting it. The aggregate equation, excluding the non-monetary gold exports, is:[1]

$$X = \$8 \cdot 2 \text{ million} + 14 \cdot 35 Y - 2 \cdot 95 P + 3 \cdot 77 C.$$
$$(2 \cdot 98) \quad (3 \cdot 86) \quad (3 \cdot 22)$$

The standard error of estimate is $31·1 million and the coefficient of multiple correlation, corrected for the number of degrees of freedom, is 0·944. This equation differs very little from the aggregate export equation including gold, which was derived in Chapter 4, except that the trend term is smaller, by approximately 50 per cent, when gold is excluded. This finding is, of course, consistent with the calculated regression for gold exports which showed them remaining very close to their trend value throughout the period. Consequently it is not necessary, in this instance, to treat gold exports separately and they have been included throughout in the export equations.

F
Canada's Current Account Credits with the United States

The behaviour of Canada's exports of goods and services in aggregate has been examined at length in Chapter 4, and this appendix will be confined to a consideration of her current accounts credits with the United States. This will provide an additional test of the theory and, moreover, by giving separate treatment to exports to the United States we shall be dealing with more than half the total value of exports of goods and services from Canada in the 1926–38 period.[1]

The general approach adopted in this appendix is modelled on that described in Chapter 4 and need not be repeated in detail. To a considerable extent the description of the derivation of the statistical series (which is considered in Appendix H) can also be applied, *mutatis mutandis*, to the present case, but there are a few questions which require special attention. It will be appropriate to review the various time series required and to discuss any problems encountered for the United States which did not arise in the aggregate case. The treatment here, as in the aggregate case, is organized in terms of the data required for the regression equation.

The published figures for Canada's balance of international payments show separately, in current dollars, Canada's transactions with the United States.[2] These published figures require adjustment, for our purposes, to exclude exports of grains and farinaceous products and to deal with the exports of whisky which, according to the trade statistics, went to the islands of St. Pierre and Miquelon during the years of prohibition in the United States.

The reasons for excluding exports of grains and farinaceous products have been discussed in Appendix D. These exports were not large and amounted, on the average, to only 2·3 per cent of Canada's total receipts from the United States on current account.[3] In the years 1934, 1935, and 1936 they were somewhat more important because of drought conditions in the western United States but, even in these years, they amounted to only about 5 per cent of the total.

The other adjustment relates to whisky. According to the trade figures, whisky exports to the United States fell to zero during this period while exports to the two small islands of St. Pierre and Miquelon rose to a value of several million dollars a year for the prohibition years and then fell back, in some years to zero and in others to a few hundred dollars, after the repeal of prohibition. To take these figures seriously would involve assumptions too bizarre to be contemplated, and the obvious solution of adding the figures for whisky exports to St. Pierre and Miquelon to the United States figures was adopted.

These two adjustments to the published data give us the figures we require, in current dollars, for this study. These figures must in turn be deflated for changes in prices and population. The current account credits for non-monetary gold, tourist and travel, and freight and shipping were deflated in a fashion identical with, or analogous to, the procedure adopted for the aggregate case.

For commodity trade this convenient solution was not possible because no price index for commodity exports to the United States separate from that for total commodity exports was available. In order to construct such an index a selection of Canada's major commodity exports was made. This selection covered an average of about 75 per cent of the total (in most years the proportion was between 70 and 80 per cent) so chosen as to provide adequate representation for all the major commodity groups. The individual commodity exports were deflated with their respective price indexes in each year and the total for each year gave the value of the sample at 1935–9 prices. The total value of the sample at current prices was divided by the value at 1935–9 prices to give a current year weighted price index for each year. This index was then used to deflate the total commodity exports. From this point on, the procedure for obtaining the value of exports of goods and services, excluding grains and farinaceous products, at 1935–9 prices and adjusted for population change followed the procedure described in Appendix H, which need not be repeated here.

The world income figure used for the aggregate case was based on the income indexes of the individual countries. The figures for the United States used in that calculation were also used in this appendix.

Of the three components of the price variable for exports to the United States, two were required for the aggregate case. The price index in the United States of goods which compete most directly with imports, appropriately weighted, was computed to provide the data required in Chapter 4 (for details, see Appendix H) and so also was the factor for the price equivalent of changes in commercial policy (likewise dealt with in Appendix H). The third component of this price variable is a Laspeyres index of the prices of exports of goods and services to the United States. The individual commodity price series used to calculate

D

the deflated value of commodity exports were combined using base period (1935–9) weights to give the required price index for commodity exports. This index in turn was combined with those for non-monetary gold, travel and shipping services, using fixed base period weights, to give the required price index for Canada's exports to the United States. These three components were used as in the aggregate case to give the relative price, adjusted for commercial policy changes, of Canada's exports to the United States.

The third explanatory variable is concerned with the supply aspects of the export relationship. It is measured by the ratio of export prices to wage rates in Canada. The ratio of the export price index (without the tariff adjustment, since exporters do not receive the proceeds of tariff imposts) to the index of wage rates in Canada gives the required series here.

The form of the regression equation is identical with that used in Chapter 4. In this appendix, as in the chapter itself, the regression analysis is based on the first differences of the respective time series. The original series and the first differences for each are shown in Table xxvii.

TABLE XXVII
ORIGINAL TIME SERIES AND FIRST DIFFERENCES REQUIRED FOR
REGRESSION ANALYSIS FOR EXPORTS TO THE UNITED STATES

	Original data				First differences			
Year	Exports (X) (millions)	Income in the US (Y)	Relative prices (P)	Supply factor (C)	X (millions)	Y	P	C
1926	606	101	111·3	124·6				
1927	631	101	113·6	121·5	+ 25	0	+ 2·3	− 3·1
1928	669	102	110·9	119·1	+ 38	+ 1	− 2·7	− 2·4
1929	691	108	108·1	114·2	+ 22	+ 6	− 2·8	− 4·9
1930	602	96	111·4	106·0	− 89	−12	+ 3·3	− 8·2
1931	521	88	115·9	100·8	− 81	− 8	+ 4·5	− 5·2
1932	424	74	110·6	98·8	− 97	−14	− 5·3	− 2·0
1933	413	73	108·7	102·8	− 11	− 1	− 1·9	+4·0
1934	477	81	105·4	106·9	+ 64	+ 8	− 3·3	+4·1
1935	549	88	96·9	102·7	+ 72	+ 7	− 8·5	−4·2
1936	661	101	95·8	101·1	+112	+13	− 1·1	−1·6
1937	730	105	96·0	98·0	+ 69	+ 4	+ 0·2	−3·1
1938	576	99	106·7	99·2	−154	− 6	+10·7	+1·2

The regression was first computed for the entire period and the equation which resulted is:

$$X = \$ -9 \cdot 2 \text{ million} + 8 \cdot 13 Y - 4 \cdot 83 P - 2 \cdot 94 C.$$
$$(1 \cdot 28) \quad (2 \cdot 05) \quad (2 \cdot 70)$$

The standard error of estimate is \$26·8 million, $R^2 = 0·896$, and $\bar{R} = 0·926$, which is significant at the 0·001 level. The von Neumann ratio is 2·41.

This equation satisfied the standard statistical tests at the significance levels (0·001 for the correlation coefficient and 0·05 for the others) which are being applied here except for the coefficient of the supply factor. For this parameter the sign of the coefficient is also perverse in terms of theoretical expectations. The behaviour of the residuals, which are presented in Table xviii, shows no clear evidence of a leading or lagged relationship or of other distortion in the equation although it will be seen that the pattern for 1937 and 1938 observed for the aggregate case is also in evidence here. If it were not for the findings in

Chapter 4 itself we might well conclude that, except for the coefficient of the supply factor, this regression is satisfactory. The results are, in general, similar to those for the aggregate case except that here it is the supply coefficient that is less satisfactory whereas in the previous case the difficulty came from the coefficient of the price term. It is important to mention too, that in both cases the income variable was clearly the dominant one; here it accounts for 73 per cent of the variance in the export variable and in the aggregate case the figure is 69 per cent. In both cases the coefficient contains its own standard error more than four times and so is significant at the 0·001 level.

In the discussion of the aggregate case it was found desirable to make a special calculation, omitting the years 1937 and 1938, because of the distortion imparted to the whole equation and reflected in the pattern of the residuals when these years were included. There was also some evidence to suggest that a major part of the effect on Canada's exports in these years originated in the United States. Consequently, we might expect to find that, for the exports to the United States taken separately, this effect would be even more pronounced. But this is not the case. For the years prior to 1937, the residuals for exports to the

TABLE XXVIII
ACTUAL VALUES, COMPUTED VALUES, AND RESIDUALS
FOR THE EXPORT VARIABLE – UNITED STATES

Year	Actual value X_a	Computed value X_c	Residual* $(X_a - X_c) = D_1$	Residual†
		(millions of dollars)		
1927	+ 25	− 11	+36	+24
1928	+ 38	+ 19	+19	+23
1929	+ 22	+ 68	−46	−31
1930	− 89	− 99	+10	+ 4
1931	− 81	− 81	0	−18
1932	− 97	− 92	− 5	+ 1
1933	− 11	− 20	+ 9	− 9
1934	+ 64	+ 60	+ 4	− 5
1935	+ 72	+101	−29	+ 4
1936	+112	+107	+ 5	+ 7
1937	+ 69	+ 31	+38	
1938	−154	−113	−41	

*From the regression analysis for the entire period.
†From the calculation which omits 1937 and 1938.

United States show six changes of sign compared with only two in the earlier calculations.

In view of the earlier analysis, to which we have referred above, it is desirable to determine the effect of omitting the two years, 1937 and 1938, by computing a second regression for the exports to the United States from which these years are dropped.

The equation which is obtained by omitting the years 1937 and 1938 and leaving the figures for the other years unchanged is:

$$X = + \$3\cdot5 \text{ million} + 7\cdot72Y - 1\cdot21P - 0\cdot06C.$$
$$(0\cdot87) \quad (1\cdot91) \quad (2\cdot01)$$

The standard error of estimate is \$16·1 million, $R^2 = 0\cdot946$, and $\bar{R} = 0\cdot958$. The von Neumann ratio is 2·24. The residuals are shown in the third column of Table XXVIII.

This equation is not very much different in its essentials from the previous one. By omitting the figures for 1937 and 1938 we have achieved a closer "fit" of the computed to the actual values as indicated by the decline in the standard error of estimate to less than two-thirds of its former value and the increase in the corrected coefficient of correlation (from 0·926 to 0·958). The constant term, which was negative in the previous equation, is now positive as it was in both the regressions for total exports.

The income coefficient has changed little but, because its standard error is less, it now contains its own standard error 8·87 times. Both of the other regression coefficients are smaller than in the previous equation and neither is now significant at the 0·05 level. The sign of the supply coefficient remains perverse (negative), but it is so small that no importance can be attached to it. The distribution of the residuals gives no cause for concern.

In general, then, this equation is more satisfactory than the first one except for the fact that the price coefficient is no longer significant at the 0·05 level.

We have found in the second equation for exports to the United States that only the income coefficient is significant at the 0·05 level. It seems worthwhile, in view of this fact and also of the emphasis that has been placed on income as an explanatory variable in the hypothesis and elsewhere in the study, to compute simple regressions with income alone as the explanatory variable.

For the entire period the equation is:

$$X = -\$1\cdot0 \text{ million} + 8\cdot92 Y.$$
$$(1\cdot40)$$

The standard error of estimate is $35·4 million, $\bar{r} + 0·887$, and the von Neumann ratio is 2·10.

For the period, excluding 1937 and 1938, the equation is:

$$X = +\$5\cdot5 \text{ million} + 7\cdot91 Y.$$
$$(0\cdot73)$$

The standard error of estimate is $17·6 million, $\bar{r} = 0·960$, and the von Neumann ratio is 2·03.

It will be observed that in both these cases the simple correlation satisfies the statistical criteria, gives a good fit, and is consistent with the theoretical expectations. This is, of course, not a general argument for replacing the more complex function by this simpler one. It is intended rather to underline the importance of income in the relationship and to show that, in some rather special cases, income alone may provide a satisfactory explanation of the behaviour of exports.

The greater importance of income as an explanatory variable in the United States is probably explained by the relatively greater fluctuations in incomes in that country. For the United States the per capita real income for the lowest year of the early 1930s was only 67 per cent of the previous peak level. For the United Kingdom the figure is 92 per cent and for the other group of countries for which figures were calculated in this study it is 91 per cent. The greater severity of the decline in income in the United States would not only tend to have greater direct effects on purchases from other countries, in this case from Canada, but, because income is such an important economic magnitude, the effects of large changes in it would tend to pervade the entire economy.

In concluding this appendix it is appropriate to summarize the most important conclusions reached in regard to Canada's exports to the United States in the period under review.

1   The general regression model gives a good estimate of the export variable measured by the standard statistical criteria. Moreover, when the results are examined year by year we find that in only one case (1927 in the first equation) do the actual and computed values of exports change in opposite directions.

2   The equation from which the years 1937 and 1938 are omitted gives a better fit than

does the equation fitted to data for the entire period. The presence of changes in expectations would seem to provide the explanation here as it does in the aggregate case.

3   Income was clearly the most important of the three explanatory variables for the United States and this was also found to be true in the aggregate analysis. In the present instance, however, the relative importance of the income factor was greater than in the previous one; income accounted for 73 per cent of the variance in the export variable in the entire period and for 92 per cent in the calculation which omitted 1937 and 1938. The corresponding figures for the aggregate regression were 69 per cent and 80 per cent respectively.

4   The other two variables were of distinctly secondary importance but nevertheless made a considerable contribution in the calculation for the entire period when they together accounted for 15 per cent of the total variance in the export variable. For the shorter period their contribution was comparatively slight; in this period they accounted for only 3 per cent of the total variance.

In summary, we find that in every instance our standard regression model has given a reasonably adequate fit to the observed data and, in every instance, income has been much the most important of the explanatory variables in the model. In some cases a simple regression using income as the sole explanatory variable may provide a satisfactory model, but it seems clear that for more general use the model which includes all three explanatory variables is preferable.

G
Canada's Demand for Imports of Goods and Services: A Disaggregated Approach

In Chapter 5 of this study we described in some detail the methods used to derive an aggregate demand function for imports of goods and services into Canada in the years 1926–38. It was there suggested that some of the limitations of the aggregate approach could be at least partially overcome if total imports were disaggregated into a number of groups and a separate equation derived for each group. It was mentioned that the advantages are by no means all on the side of disaggregation, but there is a clear gain in having the estimates on both the aggregated and the disaggregated bases, and so both approaches are used in this study. In this appendix we shall describe the disaggregation procedure and present the results of the calculations in more detail than was necessary or convenient in Chapter 5.

Part I of this appendix is devoted to a discussion of the general principles followed in carrying out the disaggregation procedure and in selecting the explanatory variables. In Part II there is a brief description of the time series used for each of the twelve groups into

D*

which the aggregate current account debits were divided. This section also includes the time series (from which the first differences required for the regression calculations were obtained) and gives the results of the calculation. A general summary and appraisal of the results of the disaggregation is contained in Chapter 5 and need not be repeated here.

PART I

The general approach used for the disaggregation is modelled on that employed in deriving the aggregate equation, i.e., we use a multiple regression of imports in each group on the relevant components of GNE and on relative prices.[1] The regressions are computed from the first differences of the time series. For commodity imports the price variable contains a special adjustment for customs tariffs which is similar in principle to that used in the aggregate equation and which is described more fully below.

Throughout this appendix we have adhered to two general principles. These we can call for convenience the principle of consistency and the principle of inclusiveness. For our purposes we can distinguish three facets to the principle of consistency. First, there is the obvious need for deriving any given time series in a consistent manner in every year of the period. Second, there is the consistency involved in maintaining the same form of the regression equation and in applying it throughout to the first differences of the various series for each of the groups.[2] Third, there is the practice of using in each case current year weighted indexes to deflate imports and components of domestic expenditure and of using base year weighted indexes[3] in the calculation of relative prices.[4]

It may appear that this principle of consistency has been applied too rigidly. If our purpose were merely to secure a good fit to the data in each case this would certainly be true; it would undoubtedly be possible to improve matters in this respect if a wider choice of explanatory variables and techniques were permitted. But such flexibility would be objectionable in the present instance for two reasons. First, it would improve the results of the regression analyses as measured by the standard statistical tests, but it would not provide a consistent test of the hypothesis and so would be unsatisfactory for our purposes. Second, if we permit ourselves a wide choice of explanatory variables we are in danger of straying further and further from testing the most acceptable theories and are apt to find ourselves using some variable for no better reason than that it gives a good fit, i.e., there is the danger that we will be developing what Yule calls "nonsense correlations." And since there is no clear, objective line of division to tell us when we are computing "nonsense correlations," it is well to apply some general principle to reduce the danger from this source. The rigorous, and possibly too rigorous, application of the principle of consistency is the price of attempting to avoid both of these pitfalls. The fact that our results have, in general, been satisfactory suggests that the price has not been too high.

The second general principle which has been applied is that of inclusiveness. This principle has two aspects which are especially relevant here. First, we have included every year of the period in each of our time series, although the practice of omitting data for some years from equations into which they do not fit well is by no means rare in work of this type.[5] Second, we have applied the principle of inclusiveness so that in every year of the period the total current account debits included in the twelve groups are exactly equal to the aggregate current account debits as reported in the official statement of the Canadian balance of payments.[6]

Total current account debits were disaggregated into twelve groups, as mentioned above. The first line of division was between commodity imports and other current account debits. The commodities were further subdivided into raw materials and manufactured goods. This division was suggested partly by the fact that raw materials are less subject to protective tariffs and partly by the arrangement of the published statistics. The raw materials total was then further divided to provide the content of our groups I and II. Group I is "food" and group II contains "all other raw materials."

A statistical difficulty was encountered in making this division between raw materials and manufactured goods. In the official trade statistics, Canadian commodity imports are subdivided into raw materials, partly manufactured goods, and fully manufactured goods. We require a two-division classification which treats all commodity imports as either raw materials or manufactured goods, and so the items classified as partly manufactured must be allocated to one of the other groups. The major items in the partly manufactured category were designated individually as either raw materials or manufactured goods on the basis of the allocation between these two categories employed in the wholesale price index which uses the two-division classification that we require. The total for the minor items in the partly manufactured group was divided between raw materials and manufactured goods in each year in the same ratio as applied for the major items which were allocated individually.

The manufactured goods total was subdivided into five groups. Here the principal criterion of allocation was the end-use of the various items. The five groups (III to VII inclusive in our classification) are: (III) consumer durables, (IV) machinery and equipment, (V) other manufactured metal products, (VI) manufactured textiles, and (VII) all other manufactured goods.

The disaggregation of the service items followed the categories in the balance of payments statement, except that interest payments were treated separately from payments on dividend account. The interest and dividends category was split for our purposes because the explanatory variables would seem to be different for these two items. The five service groups in our classification (groups VIII to XII) are: (VIII) freight and shipping, (IX) tourist and travel, (X) interest, (XI) dividends, and (XII) other service items, i.e., all other current account debits.

It was necessary to divide the total balance of payments figure for current account debits in each year among these twelve groups. For the service items this presented no difficulty since (with the minor exception noted above for freight payments after 1934) the required figures are readily available from published sources.[7]

For commodity imports the situation is slightly more complicated because the commodity trade figures, which must be used to disaggregate commodity imports, differ from the balance of payments figures for commodity trade. For our purposes the balance of payments figure is the appropriate one, and so the total figure for commodity trade in each year must be adjusted to make it equal to the balance of payments figure and the total amount of this adjustment must be distributed in some manner over the group totals for groups I–VII in our classification.

It appears that most of these adjustments required to bring the commodity trade figures to a balance of payments basis apply to imports of manufactured goods rather than to imports of raw materials.[8] The raw materials total which was derived, as explained above, from the commodity trade statement was not adjusted, and instead the entire adjustment in each year was allocated on a proportionate basis among the imports of manufactured goods. In this way the total for commodity imports included in our groups I–VII was brought into equality with the figure for commodity imports shown for each year in the statement of the balance of payments.

For ten of the twelve groups we require the per capita imports of each at 1935–9 prices.[9] The procedure was to deflate the current dollar total for each of the ten groups in each year with a current year weighted price index constructed for that group. These deflated figures were then divided by the population figure in each year to bring them to the required per capita basis.

The first of the two explanatory variables used in most of these twelve relationships was the GNE or those components of it which seemed most likely to influence imports of the particular goods or services in the group under consideration. This expenditure total was divided by a current year weighted price index and by the population figure. From this calculation we obtained the required figure of per capita expenditure in the relevant sectors at 1935–9 prices.

All the components of GNE were adjusted in each year to allow for the effects of changes in the terms of trade. The reasons for making this adjustment are developed in Appendix I and, since they are complex to explain, no attempt will be made to repeat or to summarize the argument here. The terms of trade adjustment varied from year to year, but in any one year the factor applied to the total was also applied to each of the components. In addition, as in Chapter 5, changes in inventories on farms were excluded throughout from the figure for GNE used in this appendix.

For nine of the twelve groups the second explanatory variable was the ratio of the price of imports, including the tariff in the case of commodity imports, to the appropriate index of domestic prices. The three components of the price variable (the import price index, the domestic price index, and the ratio of tariffs to value of imports) were all computed with fixed weights. In most cases the first two of these components presented no special difficulty.[10]

The third component of the price variable, the tariff factor, appears, of course, only for the seven commodity groups. The method used to make the tariff adjustment was more complex for manufactured goods than for raw materials. The more complex method will be described first and it is then a simple matter to explain the modifications required to derive the tariff factor for imports of raw materials.

The first step in deriving the tariff factor for either manufactured goods or raw materials was to total the gross ordinary duties imposed on items in the group under consideration in each fiscal year as reported in the *Trade of Canada*.[11] This total of ordinary customs duties was expressed in each case as a percentage of the total value of imports in the group.

To this ratio a tariff adjustment factor which varied from year to year but which was uniform in any one year for all five groups of manufactured goods was applied. This factor is the ratio of the "net adjusted duties" to total ordinary duties for manufactured goods in each year. The "net adjusted duties" were calculated by taking the gross ordinary duties on all manufactured goods and making the following adjustments:

1   Adding the total dumping duties imposed in each fiscal year. It was assumed that all dumping duties were imposed on manufactured goods. Since the figures for dumping duties are available only as a total and most are on manufactured goods, it seems preferable to allocate the total to manufactured goods rather than to attempt a division that would be purely arbitrary.

2   Adding the proportional share for manufactured goods of the special tax on imports which was imposed beginning in the 1932 fiscal year.

3   Deducting the proportional share for manufactured goods of duty refunds and drawbacks.

4   Adding (or deducting when it was negative) a "fixed content adjustment" to the gross ordinary duties actually imposed on manufactured goods in each year. The procedure used in deriving this "fixed content adjustment" is complex, and it is described immediately below.

The "fixed content adjustment" is required for manufactured goods because, for the price variable, a measure which can be used as the price equivalent of the tariff is needed. As an approximation to this measure the ratio of duties imposed to imports is biased because a change in the schedule of the customs duties will change the relative weights of those items for which the rate has been changed; more specifically, in the early 1930s many tariff rates were increased in order to increase their protective effect. The result is to reduce the relative weight of the items against which these protective duties have been increased, and so the increase in the average ratio of duties imposed to imports is, as a measure of the price equivalent of the tariff, biased downward in years when protective tariffs are, on balance, increased; and conversely in the case of a reduction, on balance, in the level of protective tariffs.[12]

We require a method of determining the price equivalent of the tariff on manufactured goods which will, as far as possible, be free of such bias.[13] The procedure adopted was to choose a sample which was broadly representative of all manufactured goods imports on which duties were imposed at any time during the 1926–38 period. For each of three representative years which were widely spaced through the period (the fiscal years chosen were those which were closest to the calendar years 1928, 1933, and 1938), we calculated the weight of each item in the sample as a percentage of the total imports of manufactured goods. For each item in the sample the average weight for the three years was determined and we then calculated what the gross ordinary customs duties would have been in each year if they had been imposed on imports of manufactured goods for which the proportions or relative weights remained fixed (at the average level of the three specified years) in every year of the period. The ratio was determined of the customs duties that would have been imposed on the items in the sample if the weights of the various items had remained fixed to the customs duties that were actually imposed on these items. This ratio for each year was then applied to the total gross ordinary customs duties imposed on manufactured goods to obtain an estimate of what these duties would have been if the weights of the various items had remained fixed at the average level of the three selected years.

The difference between the actual duties imposed and the duties that would have been imposed if the weights of the various items in the sample had remained constant gives the "fixed content adjustment."[14] This adjustment is added (algebraically) to the other three described above to give for each year the "total net adjusted customs duties" for imports of manufactured goods.

The ratio of total net adjusted customs duties to total gross ordinary duties imposed on imports of manufactured goods gives the tariff adjustment factor for each fiscal year. This factor, adjusted from a fiscal to a calendar year basis, is the tariff adjustment factor we require. For manufactured goods this factor varied from a low of 0·80 in 1928 to a high of 1·30 in 1933.

For each group of manufactured goods imports the percentage of total gross ordinary customs duties to value of imports in the group was adjusted by this tariff adjustment factor in each year. This gives the tariff factor required as the third component of the price variable.

For raw material imports the procedure was less complex. It was assumed that all dumping duties were applied against manufactured goods and so there was no adjustment for this item. A test which covered virtually all of the dutiable raw material imports showed that for these goods the "fixed content adjustment" would be negligible, and so no adjustment was made for this item.[15] With these two omissions the procedure used in calculating the tariff factor for imports in the two raw material groups was identical with that used for the five groups of manufactured goods imports.

The following was the general formula used to bring together in one measure the import price index for each group and the tariff adjustment:

$$P_{mt} = P_n(1+t_n)/P_0(1+t_0),$$

when P_{mt} is the import price index for items in the group under consideration with the
   tariff adjustment included,

P_0, P_n are the price indexes for the group in years 0 and n, respectively,

t_0, t_n are the tariff factors in years 0 and n, respectively.

   The final price ratio, which incorporates all three components of the price term, is of
the form P_{mt}/P_D, where P_{mt} has the meaning explained above and P_D is the relevant
domestic price index.

PART II

   A brief description of the contents of the time series used for each of the twelve groups
and the results of the regression analysis for each are given below.

Group I – Raw Materials, Food

Imports – for each year the total for "vegetable products – mainly food" was taken and
from it the value of imports of manufactured foods which were included in the total was
subtracted. To the resulting figure the total value of fishery products (nearly all of which
are food items), milk and its products, and meats was added to obtain the total value of
"raw materials, food."

Expenditure – consumer expenditure on goods and services.

Import Prices – a base period weighted price index constructed from the individual price
series for the major imports in this group.

Domestic Prices – a domestic wholesale price index of consumer goods reweighted at the
group level with import weights of consumer goods.

TABLE XXIX

GROUP I – RAW MATERIALS, FOOD

Year	Imports M (per capita)	Expenditure Y (per capita)	Relative prices P	Residual* u
1926	$5·8	$320	136	
1927	5·9	350	152	$+0·2
1928	5·8	375	150	−0·6
1929	6·8	388	127	−0·2
1930	5·5	363	131	−0·4
1931	5·6	339	111	−0·1
1932	4·7	302	111	+0·1
1933	4·2	294	110	−0·2
1934	4·7	307	113	+0·5
1935	5·0	318	107	−0·1
1936	6·0	330	103	+0·7
1937	5·7	349	104	−0·5
1938	6·5	341	92	+0·6

Regression equation – first differences

$$M = \$-0·14 + 0·023\,Y - 0·043\,P$$
$$\quad\quad\quad\;\; (0·007)\quad (0·014)$$

Standard error of estimate = $0·42, $R^2 = 0·642$, $\bar{R} = 0·750$, correlation
coefficient significant at 0·01 level, von Neumann ratio = 2·73.

*The figures in this column are derived from the actual minus the computed
value of the dependent variable in each year.

Group II – Raw Materials, Non-Food

Imports – total imports of raw materials less imports of "raw materials, food" (group I).
Expenditure – GNE as specified in Part I of this appendix.

Import Prices – a base period weighted index constructed from the individual import price series for the major commodities in this group.

Domestic Prices – an index of "raw material, non-food" prices was constructed for each of the component material groups in the domestic wholesale price index. Each of these indexes was then combined with the import weight for that component material group to give the final index of domestic prices.

TABLE XXX

GROUP II – RAW MATERIALS, NON-FOODS

Year	Imports M (per capita)	Expenditure Y (per capita)	Relative prices P	Residual u
1926	$17·6	$472	125	
1927	18·8	502	114	$+0·4
1928	19·1	541	112	−0·7
1929	19·8	537	110	+1·1
1930	17·9	488	100	0
1931	15·3	427	85	−0·4
1932	13·1	367	94	+0·1
1933	13·3	350	85	+1·0
1934	14·4	386	97	+0·2
1935	14·5	412	99	−0·4
1936	15·4	432	103	+0·5
1937	16·3	470	101	−0·1
1938	14·0	463	99	−1·7

Regression equation – first differences

$$M = -0·27 + 0·033 Y - 0·004 P$$
$$(0·007)\quad(0·039)$$

Standard error of estimate = $0·56, $R^2 = 0·721$, $\bar{R} = 0·812$, correlation coefficient significant at 0·01 level, von Neumann ratio = 1·91.

Group III – Consumer Durable Goods

Imports – furniture, radios, clocks and watches, tableware, jewelry n.o.p., 80 per cent of passenger automobiles (the proportion assigned in the *National Accounts* to consumer goods), and 60 per cent of parts for automobiles. The percentage figure used for parts was lower than for complete vehicles because some of these parts would be used for trucks and other commercial vehicles.

Expenditure – consumer expenditure on goods and services.

Import Prices – the individual import price series for furniture, motor vehicles and parts, clay and its products, and hardware and other iron and steel items were combined with fixed base period weights.

Domestic Prices – the same index as was used for group I.

Group IV – Machinery and Equipment

Imports – agricultural machinery, machinery not agricultural, engines (excluding automobile engines) and boilers, commercial vehicles and parts, 20 per cent of imports of passenger vehicles, and 40 per cent of parts for motor vehicles which could be used for either passenger vehicles or trucks.

Expenditure – domestic expenditure on machinery and equipment as reported in the *National Accounts* plus government expenditure on these items.[16]

16 Dominion-Provincial Conference on Reconstruction, *Public Investment and Capital Formation* (Ottawa, 1945), 62. Figures are given for 1926, 1929, 1930, 1933, 1937, and 1941. Figures for the other years of our period are interpolated between these years.

TABLE XXXI
GROUP III – CONSUMER DURABLE GOODS

Year	Imports M (per capita)	Expenditure Y (per capita)	Relative prices P	Residual u
1926	$ 8·1	$320	85	
1927	9·7	350	83	$ −0·1
1928	11·2	375	84	+0·3
1929	11·1	388	88	−0·3
1930	9·0	363	89	−0·4
1931	5·5	339	102	−0·8
1932	3·2	302	110	+0·7
1933	2·8	294	110	+0·3
1934	3·6	307	103	−0·4
1935	4·5	318	101	+0·3
1936	5·1	330	96	−0·3
1937	6·5	349	96	+0·5
1938	5·5	341	103	+0·3

Regression equation – first differences

$$M = \$ -0·19 + 0·058Y - 0·086P$$
$$(0·009) \quad (0·035)$$

Standard error of estimate = $0·43, $R^2 = 0·929$, $\bar{R} = 0·956$, correlation coefficient significant at 0·001 level, von Neumann ratio = 2·51.

Prices – the data which were available on domestic prices were not sufficient to permit the construction of an adequate base period weighted price index. The most satisfactory procedure in this case was to use the implicit (current year weighted) price index derived from the *National Accounts*. In order to be consistent with this approach the import price index used was also an implicit price index derived by dividing the value of imports of machinery and equipment at current prices by their value at 1935–9 prices in each year.

TABLE XXXII
GROUP IV – MACHINERY AND EQUIPMENT

Year	Imports M (per capita)	Expenditure Y (per capita)	Relative prices P	Residual u
1926	$ 7·3	$27·7	99	
1927	9·7	35·4	99	$ 0
1928	13·3	39·7	99	+2·3
1929	12·9	44·7	100	−1·9
1930	8·7	37·4	100	−1·9
1931	3·7	22·3	108	−0·1
1932	1·9	12·1	109	+1·4
1933	1·7	9·4	108	+0·7
1934	3·0	12·7	112	+0·4
1935	3·5	15·9	106	−0·6
1936	5·0	18·6	100	+0·5
1937	7·5	26·9	97	−0·1
1938	6·3	25·6	97	−0·7

Regression equation – first differences

$$M = \$ -0·03 + 0·31Y - 0·025P$$
$$(0·066) \quad (0·125)$$

Standard error of estimate = $1·17, $R^2 = 0·787$, $\bar{R} = 0·860$, correlation coefficient significant at 0·005 level, von Neumann ratio = 2·15.

Group V – *Other Manufactured Metal Products*

Imports – the residual items in the iron and its products group plus the non-ferrous metals group after deducting the items included in groups II, III, and IV.

Expenditure – GNE as specified in Part I of this appendix.

Import Prices – the United States wholesale price index for iron and steel products adjusted to Canadian dollar terms.[17]

Domestic Prices – the Canadian index of wholesale prices reweighted at the group level with import weights.

TABLE XXXIII
GROUP V – OTHER MANUFACTURED METAL PRODUCTS

Year	*Imports* M (per capita)	*Expenditure* Y (per capita)	*Relative prices* P	*Residual* u
1926	$10·2	$472	83	
1927	10·4	502	80	$−1·5
1928	13·3	541	82	+1·4
1929	15·2	537	85	+2·6
1930	9·5	488	87	−2·7
1931	4·3	427	98	−0·5
1932	1·8	367	109	+2·0
1933	2·2	350	103	+0·7
1934	4·1	386	96	−0·5
1935	5·0	412	97	−0·1
1936	5·4	432	96	−0·5
1937	6·9	470	97	−0·1
1938	4·7	463	104	−0·8

Regression equation – first differences

$$M = \$-0·21 + 0·051Y - 0·118P$$
$$\quad\quad\quad (0·016)\quad (0·108)$$

Standard error of estimate = $1·87, $R^2 = 0·742$, $\bar{R} = 0·828$, correlation coefficient significant at 0·01 level, von Neumann ratio—2·40.

Group VI – *Manufactured Textile Products*

Imports – total imports in the fibres and textiles group less the items which are classed as raw materials and included in group II.

Expenditure – consumer expenditure on goods and services.

Import prices – a base period weighted index constructed from the price series for the major items of manufactured textiles which were imported.

Domestic Prices – the domestic wholesale price of textile products which includes both textile raw materials and manufactured textiles.

Group VII – *Other Manufactured Goods*

Imports – this is the residual group for imports of manufactured goods. It includes any manufactured goods which are not included in groups III – VI inclusive.

Expenditure – GNE.

Import Prices – a base period weighted price index constructed from the individual series for manufactured goods, tea (which is classed as a manufactured good), crude peanut oil, wood and wood products, chemicals, the miscellaneous group (excluding rubber), and clay and its products.

17 Dominion Bureau of Statistics, *Export and Import Price Indexes 1926–1948*, Reference Paper No. 5 (Ottawa, 1949), 12, 27. This index was used because some 80 per cent of the total in group V consists of iron and steel manufactures, and no useful price series for imports of manufactured non-ferrous metal products are available.

Domestic Prices – the domestic wholesale price index reweighted with the import weights at the group level.

TABLE XXXIV
GROUP IV– MANUFACTURED TEXTILES

Year	Imports M (per capita)	Expenditure Y (per capita)	Relative prices P	Residual u
1926	$ 9·9	$320	104	
1927	10·4	350	99	$−0·9
1928	11·8	375	101	+1·2
1929	12·1	388	94	−0·8
1930	12·0	363	92	+1·0
1931	7·7	339	107	−0·8
1932	4·1	302	114	−0·7
1933	3·8	294	115	+0·6
1934	4·6	307	112	+0·4
1935	5·2	318	104	−0·5
1936	6·0	330	99	0
1937	6·5	349	96	−0·2
1938	5·7	341	101	+0·7

Regression equation – first differences

$$M = \$ -0·45 + 0·040Y - 0·141P$$
$$(0·015) \quad (0·048)$$

Standard error of estimate = $0·71, $R^2 = 0·827$, $\bar{R} = 0·888$, correlation coefficient significant at 0·001 level, von Neumann ratio = 3·19.

TABLE XXXV
GROUP VII – OTHER MANUFACTURED GOODS

Year	Imports M (per capita)	Expenditure Y (per capita)	Relative prices P	Residual u
1926	$16·8	$472	105	
1927	20·2	502	100	$−0·1
1928	23·4	541	95	−0·9
1929	24·8	537	93	+1·1
1930	22·9	488	95	+2·1
1931	15·6	427	98	−2·1
1932	11·0	367	99	−0·1
1933	10·3	350	98	+0·1
1934	11·5	386	99	−0·6
1935	12·9	412	100	+0·2
1936	14·4	432	100	+0·4
1937	17·0	470	100	+0·4
1938	15·9	463	100	−0·5

Regression equation – first differences

$$M = \$ -0·17 + 0·065Y - 0·35P$$
$$(0·011) \quad (0·017)$$

Standard error of estimate = $1·01, $R^2 = 0·894$, $\bar{R} = 0·933$, correlation coefficient significant at 0·001 level, von Neumann ratio = 2·70.

Group VIII – *Freight and Shipping*

Current Account Debits – as shown in the Canadian balance of international payments except that for the years after 1934 the figures are adjusted from a gross to a net basis in order to make them consistent with the figures for the period up to the end of 1934. For the years 1935–8 the reductions which this adjustment involves are, in current dollars, 6, 8, 11, and 10 million respectively.[18]

Explanatory Variables – it was assumed that expenditures for freight and shipping services would depend upon the volume of commodity imports. But commodity imports are a dependent variable in this model, and so it is appropriate to use as an explanatory variable not the volume of commodity imports but rather the explanatory variables which are relevant to these imports. These explanatory variables are the GNE and the relative price (including the tariff) of commodity imports compared with domestic prices in Canada. For the measure of domestic prices we used the Canadian wholesale price index reweighted at the group level with import weights.[19]

TABLE XXXVI
GROUP VIII – FREIGHT AND SHIPPING

Year	Current account debits M (per capita)	Expenditure Y (per capita)	Relative prices P	Residual u
1926	$10·3	$472	110	
1927	11·0	502	109	$+0·1
1928	11·4	541	110	−0·2
1929	12·4	537	108	+1·0
1930	11·3	488	103	−0·4
1931	8·0	427	106	−1·4
1932	7·1	367	110	+1·1
1933	6·8	350	106	−0·2
1934	7·7	386	104	−1·7
1935	7·9	412	101	−0·5
1936	8·7	432	100	+0·4
1937	10·1	470	100	+0·8
1938	9·1	463	99	−0·8

Regression equation – first differences

$$M = \$ -0·19 + 0·022Y - 0·116P$$
$$(0·002) \quad (0·114)$$

Standard error of estimate = $0·84, $R^2 = 0·555$, $\bar{R} = 0·675$, correlation coefficient significant at 0·025 level, von Neumann ratio = 2·38.

Group IX – Tourist and Travel

Current Account Debits – as given in the published balance of payments statements without change.

Expenditure – for the income variable we used GNE. This more comprehensive measure was used in preference to consumer expenditure because a substantial amount of foreign travel is for business purposes, and so consumer expenditure is not the only expenditure that is relevant to it.

Import Prices – a current year weighted price index applicable to expenditures by Canadians abroad on tourist and travel account. This index was supplied by the Dominion

18 Dominion Bureau of Statistics, *The Canadian Balance of International Payments*, 92–6. See also the discussion concerning this matter in Appendix H.

19 In effect for this equation we have no price term which is relevant to the dependent variable. We cannot use such a price term here because where there is competition between Canadian and other carriers we have no separate price indexes.

TABLE XXXVII
GROUP IX – TOURIST AND TRAVEL

Year	Current account debits M (per capita)	Expenditure Y (per capita)	Relative prices P	Residual u
1926	$8·5	$472	106	$−0·6
1927	8·5	502	106	−0·6
1928	8·3	541	105	−1·0
1929	9·0	537	104	+0·8
1930	7·7	488	104	−0·1
1931	6·1	427	106	−0·1
1932	4·2	367	115	−0·2
1933	4·1	350	106	+0·3
1934	4·9	386	98	−0·2
1935	6·1	412	101	+0·8
1936	7·0	432	98	+0·4
1937	7·8	470	99	+0·1
1938	7·6	463	99	0

Regression equation – first differences

$$M = \$ -0·08 + 0·022Y - 0·031P$$
$$(0·005) \quad (0·078)$$

Standard error of estimate = $·50, $R^2 = 0·750$, $\bar{R} = 0·833$, correlation coefficient significant at 0·01 level, von Neumann ratio = 2·18.

TABLE XXXVIII
GROUP X – INTEREST*

Year	Current account debits M	Security sales† S	Residual u
1926	$145		
1927	151	$+141	$+1
1928	160	+111	+5
1929	164	+108	0
1930	171	+249	−4
1931	180	+163	−3
1932	172	+ 3	−6
1933	169	− 14	−1
1934	168	− 42	+3
1935	155	− 95	−7
1936	156	−140	−9
1937	142	−114	−7
1938	139	− 92	+3

Regression equation (using first differences in M as dependent variable and S as independent variable)

$$M = \$1·64 + 0·049S$$
$$(0·013)$$

Standard error of estimate $4·9, $r^2 = 0·595$, $\bar{r} = 0·744$, correlation coefficient significant at 0·005 level, von Neumann ratio = 1·21 (this ratio is slightly above the level which would indicate positive serial correlation at the 0·05 level in the residuals).

*Figures in this table are in millions of current dollars.
†Average net sales of securities abroad in current and preceding year (in millions of current dollars).

Bureau of Statistics and, since we have not the individual price series from which it was calculated, it is not possible to compute a base period weighted index for this group. Domestic Prices – the implicit (current year weighted) price index for GNE. A current year weighted domestic price index is used in order to be consistent with the use of a current year weighted price index for the numerator of the price term.

Group X – *Interest*

Current Account Debits – interest payments as derived from the balance of payments up to the end of 1936.[20] For the 1937 and 1938 figures the dividends paid to non-residents were deducted from total interest and dividend payments to obtain the figure for interest payments. These figures for interest payments were not deflated for price changes nor were they put on a per capita basis for purposes of computing the regression equation.

Explanatory Variables – the change in interest payments made to non-residents will depend partly on the changes in external holdings of Canadian debt securities and partly on changes in the average rate of interest paid on these securities. For the change in the former we took the average of the net new sales of securities to non-residents in the current and in the preceding year. The figure for the preceding year was taken into account because of the lag between the issue of a new (or the retirement of an old) security and the appearance of a change in the interest item in the balance of payments. In the absence of any adequate index of the interest rate paid on outstanding securities which were held abroad, no variable to represent this factor was included in the regression equation.

Comparability with Other Groups – The figures for interest payments used in the regression analysis were in current dollars and were not on a per capita basis. It was necessary, for the summary of the residuals in Chapter 5, to put all of them in the same units. The residuals for this group in each year were divided by the population and the resulting per capita figure was deflated by the implicit price index applicable to total current account debits.

Group XI – *Dividends*

Current Account Debits – the figure for dividends paid abroad.[21] For the regression analysis this figure was not deflated for price changes nor was it put on a per capita basis. Explanatory Variables – dividend payments depend principally upon profits after taxes in the recent past, and, probably to a lesser extent, on views as to future prospects. In addition, dividends must come from profits, and so the appropriate explanatory variable is the total profits (after taxes) of those companies which had profits in the recent past. This figure was estimated by taking the total federal corporation tax liabilities[22] for each year and dividing by the tax rate on corporation profits in that year. This gave an estimate of the total profits of companies which had profits in each year. When federal and provincial taxes on these profits[23] are deducted we have an estimate of the profit figure we require.

A multiple regression of dividend payments to non-residents on corporation profits after taxes of the profit companies for the current year and the two preceding years was computed. Profits in the current year were found to have a negligible influence, and so this

20 *Ibid.*, 97.
21 *Ibid.*
22 *National Accounts*, Table 50, p. 92. This estimate is more accurate for the prewar period than it would be for the postwar period because, prior to World War II, there was no provision for loss carryover in the tax legislation.
23 *Ibid.*

TABLE XXXIX
GROUP XI – DIVIDENDS*

Year	Current account debits M	R_1	R_2	Residual u
1926	$ 95	$291†	$270‡	
1927	106	361	291	$– 5
1928	115	400	361	– 8
1929	158	480	400	+24
1930	177	502	480	+ 3
1931	150	320	502	– 7
1932	130	227	320	+11
1933	95	184	227	–18
1934	100	219	184	+13
1935	115	289	219	– 2
1936	155	302	289	+28
1937	160	390	302	–12
1938	168	479	390	–17

Regression equation – first differences

$$M = \$ + 3 \cdot 25 + 0 \cdot 143 R_1 + 0 \cdot 119 R_2$$
$$(0 \cdot 067) \quad (0 \cdot 070)$$

Standard error of estimate = $14·13, $R^2 = 0 \cdot 608$, $\bar{R} = 0 \cdot 722$, correlation coefficient significant at 0·025 level, von Neumann ratio = 2·60.

*Figures in this table are in millions of current dollars.
†Estimated profits after taxation of Canadian corporations which made profits in year $N - 1$.
‡Estimated profits after taxation of Canadian corporations which made profits in year $N - 2$.

TABLE XL
GROUP XII – OTHER SERVICES

Year	Current account debits M (per capita)	Residual u
1926	$ 9·6	
1927	9·8	$+0·2
1928	10·3	+0·5
1929	10·1	–0·2
1930	10·6	+0·5
1931	8·5	–2·1
1932	9·0	+0·5
1933	9·1	+0·1
1934	6·9	–2·2
1935	7·6	+0·7
1936	8·5	+0·9
1937	9·3	+0·8
1938	10·3	+1·0

No satisfactory explanation for the behaviour of this group could be developed. See comments in text.

variable was dropped and the explanatory variables retained related to the estimated profits after taxes of the profit companies in the two prior years were retained.[24]

Comparability with Other Groups – The problem that arises here is identical with that already discussed in connection with interest payments (group X) and the same solution was adopted.

Group XII – *Other Services*

Current Account Debits – the total for "all other current account debits" as reported in the balance of payments. The principal items are immigrants' remittances, government expenditures abroad, and film rentals. The total was deflated with the implicit price index for total current account debits.

Explanatory Variables – the total for this group behaved in such an erratic manner that it was impossible to obtain a first difference correlation coefficient to which any acceptable degree of significance could be attached. The sources of the difficulty appear to lie partly in the heterogeneous nature of this group and partly in the complex of factors which account for the lags in the changes in the various components behind the changes in GNE or other explanatory variables. In addition, the statistics for the items in this group are, in general, less accurate than for the other groups.[25] It was, therefore, assumed that for every year the first difference would be zero, i.e., that the best forecast of the figure for the succeeding year would be that it would remain unchanged from its level in the current year.

24 Other explanatory variables which might have been used are, for example, the exchange rate, investment plans, and changes in the relative distribution of profits between different industries. These additional variables would seem to have been important in only a few years of the period or to be difficult to express in quantitative terms. In view of these difficulties and also the technical statistical problems (multicollinearity and loss of degrees of freedom) which would be involved if additional explanatory variables were added, it was decided to use only the two explanatory variables mentioned in the text.

25 Dominion Bureau of Statistics, *The Canadian Balance of International Payments,* Ch. XIV.

H
Derivation of Time Series required for the Export Equations

In Chapter 4 we saw that, for the determination of the export equation, we required the time series for each of four variables. These are the dependent variable (exports of goods and services, excluding, for reasons considered in Appendix D, grains and farinaceous products) and the three independent or explanatory variables (income in other countries, the price of Canada's exports relative to prices in the importing countries, and the price of Canada's exports relative to domestic costs of production). In this appendix we describe the derivation of these time series.

For the dependent variable there is required a measure of Canada's exports of goods and services, including non-monetary gold but excluding grains and farinaceous products, for each year of the period 1926–38.

The starting point here is obviously the figure for total current account credits for each year as shown in Canada's balance of international payments.[1] These figures may be accepted, except for an adjustment to the freights and shipping account, as the value in current dollars of Canada's exports of goods and services. This adjustment is necessary because the reporting of these figures was changed, beginning in 1935, from a net to a gross basis.[2] It is necessary that the figures be on a consistent basis throughout the period we are considering and, therefore, the statistics for the years after 1934 are reduced to make them comparable with those for earlier years. The required reductions were estimated for the years 1935–9 at $6, $8, $11, $10, and $13 million respectively.

The published balance of payments figures, with the freight and shipping account adjusted to put it on a consistent basis throughout the period and with exports of grains and farinaceous products deducted, give us the total current dollar export figures we require for purposes of testing the hypothesis. These figures must be deflated for price changes, since the hypothesis was developed in "real" terms; and they must also be adjusted to take account of population change.

The price deflation is the more complex question and will be dealt with first. We want to know what the value of exports would have been in each year if they had been valued at 1935–9 prices and, therefore, it is appropriate to deflate the current dollar figures with a price index using current year weights.

For commodity exports and for some of the service items such an index was readily obtained. A Paasche type index for commodity exports was kindly made available by the International Payments Division of the Dominion Bureau of Statistics. Total commodity exports were deflated with this index. Exports of grains and farinaceous products were deflated with a current year weighted price index constructed from individual indexes for wheat, wheat flour, and barley, which account for most of the exports in this group. The deflated figures for grains and farinaceous products were deducted from the deflated figures for total commodity exports to give the values at 1935–9 prices of commodity exports as the term is used in this appendix, i.e., excluding grains and farinaceous products.

Exports of non-monetary gold are shown separately from other commodity exports in the Canadian balance of payments figures. The figures for gold exports were deflated by an index of the price of gold in Canadian dollars computed on the base 1935–9=100.

Receipts on tourist and travel account were deflated with a price index calculated by the Dominion Bureau of Statistics and made available for purposes of this study.

The deflation of receipts on freight and shipping account was a more troublesome problem. Each of the three components of this item (ocean freight, rail freight on exports, and freight on goods in transit through Canada) was divided by the related price index. Ocean freight receipts were deflated by the *Economist* index of tramp shipping rates (converted to Canadian dollar terms and to the base 1935–9=100). For rail freight on exports and on "in transit" traffic, an index computed from average railway revenue per ton-mile of freight carried was calculated and this index was used to deflate these two items.[3] The sum of the deflated ocean and rail freight receipts gave the total figure for receipts on freight and shipping account at 1935–9 prices.[4]

The total value of the items considered above at current prices was then divided by their total value at 1935–9 prices to give a simple current year weighted price index. This index, which appears in Table XLI, column 4 was then used to deflate the relevant figure for current account credits for each year.

TABLE XLI
CANADA'S CURRENT ACCOUNT CREDITS 1926–38

Year	Total current account credits	Grains etc.	Total less grains etc.	Price index (1935–9= 100)	Total less grains at 1935–9 prices	Population index	Total exports less grains adjusted for population and at 1935–9 prices
(all dollar figures in millions)							
1926	$1,665	$481	$1,184	126·6	$935	100·0	$ 935
1927	1,633	447	1,186	124·7	951	101·2	940
1928	1,788	558	1,230	122·5	1,004	102·3	981
1929	1,646	333	1,313	121·2	1,083	103·4	1,047
1930	1,297	235	1,062	113·1	939	104·4	899
1931	972	162	810	98·9	819	105·2	779
1932	808	167	641	89·1	719	105·9	679
1933	829	156	673	88·5	760	106·6	712
1934	1,020	174	846	93·6	904	107·3	843
1935	1,139	180	959	95·2	1,007	107·9	933
1936	1,422	284	1,138	96·6	1,178	108·7	1,084
1937	1,582	176	1,406	104·6	1,344	109·3	1,230
1938	1,351	132	1,219	101·8	1,197	110·2	1,086

Sources: Dominion Bureau of Statistics, *The Canadian Balance of International Payments 1926 to 1948* (Ottawa 1949), 154, 158. The figures for freight credits have been adjusted in the years 1935 to 1938 as described in the text. *Trade of Canada*, various years.

It is also necessary to adjust the deflated export figures to take account of population change in the importing countries. For this purpose an index of world population was constructed by dividing the rest of the world into three parts – the United States, the United Kingdom, and all other countries. For the United States and the United Kingdom the population figures in each year were expressed as percentages of the 1926 population. For the rest of the world the population figures for the seven countries which were the largest purchasers of Canadian goods (excluding grains and farinaceous products) were used.[5] For each country, the population in each year, expressed as a percentage of its 1926 population, was weighted in proportion to that country's average purchases from Canada in the period. The aggregate so computed was used to give the population index for the countries other than the United States and the United Kingdom. Then the final population index was computed by weighting the three separate indexes in proportion to the purchases of goods and services from Canada by each of the three. The value of Canada's exports at 1935–9 prices was divided by the population index to give the final figure for exports in each year at 1935–9 prices adjusted for changes in population in the rest of the world.

Table XLI shows the results of the major steps in the deflation process and, in the last column, the figures required for exports to test the hypothesis of Chapter 1.

The first of the three explanatory variables used in the regression equation is the level of income in the rest of the world, i.e., the real income, adjusted for population change, in countries other than Canada. The starting point was the real income of each country for each of the years 1926–38 inclusive.[6] For the United States and the United Kingdom[7] the income figure in real terms[8] in each year was expressed as a percentage of the 1935–9 average. The remaining countries were represented by the same seven countries as were included in constructing the world population index described above. For each of these countries the real income in each year was expressed as a percentage of the 1935–9 average national income for that country. These percentage figures were then combined to form an

TABLE XLII
INDEX OF REAL INCOME IN THE REST OF THE WORLD
(all figures have been adjusted for population change)

Year	United States	United Kingdom*	Other†	Index‡
1926	101·2	84·0	81·0	93·7
1927	101·5	88·3	84·0	95·4
1928	102·0	88·1	86·1	98·0
1929	108·1	88·7	84·8	99·6
1930	96·3	89·9	81·4	92·0
1931	87·9	84·7	78·3	85·3
1932	73·5	83·1	78·5	76·4
1933	72·8	87·0	83·9	77·9
1934	80·9	91·2	86·7	84·1
1935	88·4	96·6	90·9	90·5
1936	100·9	100·3	96·9	100·0
1937	105·4	101·9	101·3	103·9
1938	99·2	99·6	103·6	100·2

*Clark's table is headed "Great Britain," but the figures used here were taken from line 4 of his table, which is for the United Kingdom.
†Australia, New Zealand, South Africa, France, Germany, The Netherlands, and Japan weighted in proportion to purchases from Canada.
‡Computed with weights United States 60, United Kingdom 20, Other 20.

Sources: Colin Clark, *The Conditions of Economic Progress*, 3rd ed. (Macmillan 1957), Ch. III; League of Nations, *Statistical Yearbook*, various years.

index, the weight given to each country being proportional to its importance in Canada's commodity export trade (excluding, of course, grains and farinaceous products). The figures for the United States and the United Kingdom (also weighted in accordance with their respective importance in Canada's export trade) were combined with the index for the other seven countries to provide the appropriately weighted index of total world income. This index of total income was then divided by the world population index and the resulting figures were adjusted proportionately in each year so that the 1935–9 average was 100·0.[9]

The relative price of exports is the second explanatory variable in the regression equation. This variable is included because of the general presumption that, *ceteris paribus*, if the relative price of exports rises a smaller quantity will be purchased, and *vice versa*. For purposes of this study we require the relative price (including the price equivalent of the tariff and other elements of commercial policy in the importing countries) of Canada's exports compared with the relevant index of domestic prices in these other countries.

The price variable has, therefore, three components: the price index for exports of goods and services, the special adjustment for customs duties and other barriers to Canada's trade imposed by other countries, and the appropriate measure of domestic prices in these other countries. A base period weighted measure was used for each of the components of this variable. This was necessary because the price indexes in the importing countries are of the Laspeyres type and so the other components should be of a similar type. An additional reason for using fixed weight indexes here is provided by the special problems that arise in computing the factor to take account of commercial policy changes in the importing countries.

For the first of the three components of the price variable we require a Laspeyres price index for Canada's exports. Such a price index for all commodity exports has been published[10] and, when the grain and farinaceous products constituents have been removed, the resulting index covers the commodity trade with which we are concerned. Price indexes for gold, tourist and travel, and the three components of the freight and shipping items have already been used to deflate these items. All these separate indexes, given fixed weights based on the average relative importance of the various items for the years 1935–9, were combined to give the total index for exports.

The second component of the price variable is the price level in other countries for items that compete with purchases from Canada. No single price index will meet all the varied and sometimes conflicting criteria[11] and we shall use the single price index which seems to come as close as is possible in practice to meeting the theoretical requirements.

The general approach was to derive the domestic price index in each of the United States, United Kingdom, and other countries for the items in those countries which competed most closely with imports from Canada. These three separate indexes were then combined in the fashion described below to make the required index of domestic prices in the purchasing countries.

For the United States the domestic price index for commodities was calculated by taking the wholesale price indexes for foods and for raw materials since such a large percentage of Canada's commodity exports falls into these categories. These two indexes were weighted in proportion to the relative importance of imports from Canada in these two categories in the period 1935–9. To determine the proportions, a sample which covered some 75 per cent of Canada's commodity exports to the United States was analysed. This price index was combined with the United States price indexes for non-monetary gold, tourist and travel, and freight and shipping, each weighted in proportion to its relative importance in Canada's exports to the United States in the 1935–9 period. The index which resulted from these calculations was converted from United States to Canadian dollars to make it comparable with the Canadian price index and then adjusted proportionately in each year to make the 1935–9 average equal to 100·0.

For the United Kingdom a similar procedure was used except that only commodity prices were included in this index. Imports of goods from Canada were analysed as for the United States and again found to consist almost entirely of foods and raw materials. The relative weight of each of these in the 1935–9 period was calculated and the commodity price index for the United Kingdom was constructed by combining the wholesale price indexes for food and raw materials with weights determined by the relative importance of these two classes of goods in exports from Canada to the United Kingdom in the 1935–9 period. Only commodity prices were used in this index but commodities were 84 per cent of Canada's total current account credits (excluding grains and farinaceous products) with the United Kingdom in this period. This index, converted to Canadian dollar terms and to the base 1935–9=100, was used as the measure of the domestic price level in the United Kingdom of items which competed with imports from Canada.

For the remaining countries a sample of some 75 per cent of Canada's exports to them was analysed into food, raw materials, and manufactured goods. The world price index of each of these three groups was then weighted according to its relative importance in Canada's trade with these countries in the years 1935–9.[12] The resulting index, adjusted for exchange rates and to make the average 1935–9 index figure equal to 100·0, was taken as the appropriate measure of domestic prices in these countries.

The three domestic price indexes (for the United States, the United Kingdom, and other countries) were then combined into a single index by weighting each of the three in proportion to the relative importance of Canada's current account credits (excluding grains and farinaceous products) with each. The weights used were 60, 20, and 20 per cent, respectively, and these were within one or two percentage points not only of the shares in 1935–9 but also of those for the entire period 1926–38. This combined index of the three separate domestic price indexes, each computed with weights determined by the composition of imports from Canada, was used as the measure of prices in the rest of the world.

The third and last element in the price variable is the adjustment for changes in commercial policy. This is another troublesome problem and it would be difficult to deal with if only one country were involved and if changes in the rates of customs duties were the only commercial policy measure employed. Even in this simplified case the problem would be complicated by the fact that tariffs are not increased uniformly for all goods and that even if they were, the effect would vary greatly for different types of goods.[13] When we consider the additional facts that many countries are involved and that other measures in addition to tariff changes were used to influence the course of trade in this period, the impossibility of computing any precise quantitative measure of the price equivalent of commercial policy changes is obvious. But commercial policy was important in international trade in our period and an attempt to compute an approximation to the price equivalent of changes in it must be made.

In making the estimate for the price equivalent of the United States tariff the first step was to take total customs duties collected by the United States in each year as a percentage of her commodity imports in the year. The figure varied from a minimum of 13·3 per cent in 1928 to a maximum of 19·8 per cent in 1933.[14] It was assumed that this rate would also apply to imports from Canada. This assumption seems not unreasonable because United States total imports are made up largely of foods and raw materials and this is also true of her imports from Canada. We can be reasonably certain at least that the trends in the total ratio will be similar to the trends in the ratio for imports from Canada, and it seems probable that the absolute levels will not differ greatly. In any event this procedure is forced upon us because we do not have separate figures for customs duties on imports from Canada and it is fortunate that the ratio for total imports provides what would seem likely to be a reasonably satisfactory guide to the ratio for imports from Canada.

Customs tariffs apply only to trade in goods and we are concerned with both goods and services. Therefore, the ratio for customs duties to commodity imports has to be reduced to relate customs duties to imports of goods and services combined. In three representative years (1928, 1933, and 1938) Canada's commodity exports to the United States averaged 46 per cent of her exports of goods and services to that country. Therefore, the tariff ratio for Canada's exports of goods and services to the United States was taken in each year to be 46 per cent of the ratio of customs tariff to total United States imports.[15]

This tariff adjustment factor must be incorporated in the price of exports to the United

States since the tariff adds to the cost of imports and so weakens their competitive position in comparison with domestic goods. The procedure used was to increase the price index for exports to the United States by a factor computed as 46 per cent of the ratio of customs duties to commodity imports for that year. The price indexes which resulted from this calculation were then adjusted proportionately in each year to make the average for the 1935-9 period equal to 100·0. The series which resulted gives the price index, adjusted for United States tariffs, of Canada's exports of goods and services to that country.

No adjustment was made in the price indexes for exports to countries other than the United States. The principal reason for this arises from the major shift in Canada's trade pattern which occurred during our period and which coincided with the period of most rapid change in the levels of custom tariffs in the great majority of countries. The early 1930s saw general and very sharp increases in the rates of customs duties, and in this same period the system of Imperial Preference which resulted from the Ottawa Agreements of 1932 became of much greater importance in Canada's trade.[16] For example, in 1929, Canada sold 12 per cent of her exports of goods and services (excluding grains and farinaceous products) to the United Kingdom; in 1933 this figure had increased to 22 per cent. Over the same period exports to countries other than the United States and the United Kingdom fell from 19 per cent to 17 per cent. In part the relative increase in exports to the United Kingdom may be explained by the earlier and more rapid recovery in incomes there, but there is no doubt that commercial policy was a major factor in the change. The difficulty of determining a price equivalent of commercial policy changes in such circumstances is obvious. The procedure used here is equivalent to assuming that the favourable effects on Canada's exports to the United Kingdom as a result of the change in that country's commercial policy was just offset by the adverse effects of commercial policy changes in countries other than the United States and the United Kingdom. This, it can safely be said, understates the net adverse effect of commercial policies in countries other than the United States, but there are no firm grounds for an adjustment to offset this known bias.

TABLE XLIII
PRICE OF CANADA'S EXPORTS RELATIVE TO DOMESTIC PRICES
IN THE REST OF THE WORLD (all price indexes on base 1935-9=100)

Year	Price index for Canada's exports (P_x)*	Domestic price indexes			Total for rest of world (Pf)	Relative prices of exports adjusted for tariff rates
		United States	United Kingdom	Other countries		
1926	128·7	110·2	136·2	146·3	122·6	105·0
1927	125·6	107·7	132·8	137·0	118·6	105·9
1928	123·4	109·0	129·6	134·0	118·1	104·5
1929	123·0	109·2	125·2	129·9	116·5	105·6
1930	109·1	99·6	104·3	111·0	102·8	106·1
1931	97·8	89·1	86·0	91·2	88·9	110·0
1932	89·9	85·7	70·7	77·0	81·0	111·0
1933	89·7	86·1	81·2	85·0	84·9	105·7
1934	94·2	92·7	90·5	95·0	92·7	101·6
1935	94·9	99·3	92·2	93·9	96·8	98·0
1936	98·0	100·3	98·0	97·9	99·4	98·6
1937	105·3	103·9	113·2	113·6	107·7	97·8
1938	101·6	97·4	99·5	103·1	99·0	102·6

* Including adjustment for tariffs imposed in the importing countries.

Sources: United States Government Printing Office. *Statistical Abstract of the United States,* various years; *Journal of the Royal Statistical Society.* Vol. 103 (1940), 349; W. A. Lewis, *World Production, Prices and Trade, 1870-1960* (Manchester School, May 1952), 118; W. S. Woytinsky and E. S. Woytinsky, *World Commerce and Governments – Trends and Outlook* (New York: Twentieth Century Fund, 1955), 263-4.

This tariff adjustment factor, crude as it is, will nevertheless show correctly the *direction* of change in commercial policy, and, moreover, it will show strong movements in years when the trend of change was strong and smaller changes in years of less pronounced change.[17] The adjustment factor we have used is based only on United States data, but the economic influences which affect commercial policy in that country were not, in general, different from those that were felt in other countries and the response to these influences, while it differed in degree from country to country, was generally similar in trend for the United States and for other countries.[18]

The third, and last, of the explanatory variables in the equation is that concerned with the supply side of the relationship. The measure we require for this supply factor is the ratio of export prices to domestic costs in Canada. We have already computed an index of export prices,[19] and the additional information we require is concerned with costs in Canada. For this purpose we shall use the index of wage rates in Canada. Not only are wages by far the most important cost item, but other costs which are relevant to short run decisions of producers are also likely to be more or less close reflections of wage levels. It would be preferable to use an index for all wage rates rather than one confined to the export industries even if it were possible to overcome the formidable difficulties in the way of computing such an index. Export industries have costs for materials, services, etc., apart from wages and these other costs will be affected by wage rates in other sectors of the economy. Thus, by using a general index of wage rates we, in effect, give some weight to the non-wage variable costs of the export industries. Of perhaps greater importance from a statistical viewpoint is the fact that the index of wage rates tended to fluctuate very similarly for the major industrial groupings,[20] with the result that an index of wage rates in the export industries would differ but little from an index of wage rates for all industries. The supply factor in the regression equation can, therefore, be very satisfactorily represented by the ratio of Canadian export prices to wage rates in Canada.

TABLE XLIV
EXPORT PRICES AND DOMESTIC WAGE RATES IN
CANADA (all indexes on base 1935–9=100)

Year	Index of export prices*	Index of wage rates in Canada	Index of ratio of export prices to wage rates
1926	130·1	99·4	130·9
1927	126·8	101·5	124·9
1928	124·9	102·7	121·6
1929	124·4	104·5	119·1
1930	109·7	105·2	104·3
1931	97·1	101·7	95·5
1932	88·6	94·5	93·8
1933	88·3	89·6	98·6
1934	93·3	90·5	103·1
1935	94·3	93·1	101·3
1936	97·8	94·8	103·2
1937	105·5	101·8	103·6
1938	101·9	104·9	97·1

*These figures exclude the tariff adjustment because we are here interested in the return to the seller, not the cost to the buyer.

Sources: Bank of Canada, *Statistical Summary, 1946 Supplement,* 107.

I
Derivation of the Time Series Required for the Import Equations

The derivation of the time series used in the equation for current account debits was, if anything, more complex and more tedious than for current account credits. Consequently, it seems appropriate in this case, as in that of current account credits, to discuss such matters in an appendix rather than in the body of the book.

For the dependent variable, imports of goods and services, it is necessary to determine the value in constant prices and on a per capita basis in each of the years 1926-38 inclusive. The obvious starting point is the balance of payments figure for current account debits.[1] This figure is deflated with a price index and the deflated figure is then divided by the population total in each year to give the final figure for imports of goods and services per capita at 1935-9 prices.

The major problem here is the derivation of an appropriate price index. This involves both deciding on the type of price index to be used and securing the data necessary to compute it. Since the object is to determine what the value of imports in each year at 1935-9 prices would have been, the use of a current year weighted price index is indicated. In addition, the most satisfactory income data expressed in terms of constant dollars (those provided in the *National Accounts*) are, in effect, derived from current year weighted price indexes, and it is desirable to apply the same type of index to the deflation of imports as that applied to the deflation of income.[2] For both these reasons a current year weighted price index is preferable.

Once we decide to use a current year weighted price index our next problem is to secure the necessary data and compute the index. Commodity imports and tourist and travel expenditures, as reported in the balance of international payments, are deflated by their respective current year weighted price indexes.[3] For freight and shipping debits, a price index derived by combining the *Economist* index of tramp shipping rates, average freight per ton of coal imported from the United States, and average revenue per ton-mile of freight carried by class I railroads in the United States was constructed. These three subindexes (commodities, tourist and travel, and freight and shipping) were then used to compute the required current year weighted price index.

The current account debits in the balance of payments were deflated with the price index described above to give their value at 1935-9 prices. This deflated figure was then divided by the figure for population in each year to arrive at the per capita current account debits at 1935-9 prices. This gives us the data for the dependent variable (M) in the import equation.

We turn next to consider the explanatory (independent) variables in the equation, viz., per capita real income in Canada and the price of imports compared with domestic prices. We shall deal first with the income variable and, for data on this, the obvious source is the *National Accounts*, where, in Table 5, we find GNE in constant (1949) dollars.[4] For our purposes four adjustments are made to the figures given in this table. The components are converted from the 1949 price basis to the 1935-9 basis, changes in inventories on farms are excluded, there is an adjustment for changes in the terms of trade, and the data are converted from an aggregate to a per capita basis. The first and last of these adjustments are purely mechanical operations and require no further discussion. The second and third items cannot be dismissed so easily.

The GNE includes the figure for changes in inventories on farms so that an increase in these inventories is a positive factor in the GNE for the period and a decrease enters as a deduction. From an accounting standpoint this procedure is unexceptionable, but it seems less appropriate in arriving at the measure of income which is relevant for our present purposes. We are concerned with expenditure, and it does not seem helpful for our purposes to regard an increase in farm inventories as an expenditure by farmers. The more appropriate assumption here is that the expenditure will be made when the product has been sold rather than when it has been added to inventory. In fact, the total volume of inventories on farms was not very much different at the end of 1938 than it was at the beginning of 1926, and so the effect of this adjustment on the average level of income is negligible although the effect on year-to-year fluctuations is appreciable in a few years.[5]

The second adjustment to the income figure is that required to take into account changes in the terms of trade. In the constant dollar figures in the *National Accounts*, the current account credits and current account debits have been valued at their respective 1935–9 average prices. These deflated figures show what current account credits, current account debits, and the net foreign balance would have been in each year if prices had remained constant at their 1935–9 average level. If, however, we take the difference between these two figures in any year to represent the purchasing power of the net foreign balance we introduce the implicit assumption that there has been no change in the terms of trade in that year compared with the base period. Since significant changes in the terms of trade did occur during the 1926–38 period, it is necessary to make adjustments in the constant dollar figures to take account of such changes.

The values of current account credits and of current account debits, respectively, at current prices do reflect changes in the terms of trade and the difference between them gives the actual purchasing power, at current prices, of the net foreign balance in any year. If this net foreign balance is deflated by the appropriate price index we have a measure of the purchasing power, at 1935–9 prices, of the net foreign balance in any year. And, since the current dollar balance was derived from current dollar value figures, this measure reflects the effect of changes in the terms of trade from year to year.

The adjustment required is that which will measure the difference between Canada's net position on international account as it actually was in any year compared with what it would have been if the terms of trade had remained unchanged at the 1935–9 average level. The actual net position (in real terms) is shown if we deflate the current dollar balance by the appropriate price index. The position as it would have been if the terms of trade had remained throughout at the 1935–9 level is shown by the difference between current account credits valued at 1935–9 prices and current account debits valued at 1935–9 prices. The difference between the deflated current dollar balance and what the balance would have been if all prices had remained at 1935–9 levels (the assumption involved in the standard deflation procedure) gives the adjustment required to take into account changes in the terms of trade.

The most troublesome problem arises in deciding what price index should be used to deflate the current dollar balance. If, for example, the balance in a particular year is active this may be interpreted to mean that the country can in the future pay for a larger volume of imports than would have been possible if it had not had the active balance; alternatively, we may look upon the active balance as permitting the consumption of a given amount of imports in future in return for a smaller future volume of exports. The first viewpoint suggests that we should deflate the net foreign balance with the index of the prices of imports of goods and services; the second suggests we should deflate it with the price index for exports of goods and services.[6]

There appears, in principle, to be no means of resolving this dilemma but fortunately the difficulty turns out to have been of slight importance quantitatively in the 1926–38 period. In years when the price indexes of imports and exports differed by a relatively large amount the net foreign balance was small, and in years when the net foreign balance was large the difference between the two price indices was slight. In these circumstances it seemed most reasonable to deflate an active balance with the index of import prices and to deflate a passive balance with the index of export prices.[7]

The figure for the terms of trade adjustment was computed for each year in the manner described above. The percentage relationship of this adjustment to the GNE at 1935–9 prices was determined for each year and each of the components of GNE was adjusted by this percentage. The adjustment varied from a maximum positive figure of $40 million, of 0·8 per cent of GNE, in 1927 to a maximum negative figure of $91 million, or 2·3 per cent or GNE, in 1932.

The relative prices of imports is the second explanatory variable in our equation.[8] This variable is included because of the general presumption that, *ceteris paribus*, if relative price rises, a smaller quantity will be purchased, and *vice versa*. For purposes of this study we require the relative price (including the tariff) of imports of goods and services compared with the relevant index of domestic prices in Canada.

The price variable has, therefore, three components: the price index for imports of goods and services, the adjustment factor to take account of customs duties and other levies that are applied against imports but not against similar items of domestic origin, and the appropriate measure of the domestic price level. A base period weighted measure was used in all three cases. For reasons explained below, the tariff adjustment factor must be computed with fixed weights and this makes it desirable that the other indexes also be of this type.

A base year weighted price index for commodity imports has been published for each year of the period 1926–48.[9] The three components of the freight and shipping price index (calculated as described earlier in this appendix) and the tourist and travel price index were each given the fixed weights indicated by average experience in the five years 1935–9, inclusive. These were all combined using fixed weights to make the index of import prices.[10]

Domestic prices are the second of the three components of the price variable in the import equation. The theory of demand leads us to expect that it would be the relative prices of imports (including the tariff) compared with domestic prices that will be the measure of the relevant price variable, and so, for our measure of domestic prices, we require an index appropriate to determining the relative price of imports of goods and services compared with domestic prices.

This is a very troublesome question and no single answer can be considered entirely satisfactory.[11] We might take the domestic wholesale price index as Harberger[12] does, but such a procedure would be less satisfactory for Canada than it is for the United States because of the large weight assigned to goods such as wheat and base metals, of which the major part of Canadian production is exported. It is true that a change in the prices of such export goods will have an effect on Canada's imports indirectly through the changes that will be induced in domestic incomes and in other prices. But the *direct* effect of, for example, an increase in the price of wheat in leading to the substitution of imported goods for domestic goods seems likely to be negligible, since Canada is not likely to be importing any large quantity of wheat in any case. And the same argument applies to other major export products which are heavily weighted in the domestic wholesale price index, but which are an insignificant proportion of imports.

The implication of the above discussion is that the most appropriate price variable would be one constructed from domestic prices, weighted according to the relative import-ance of imports in each category.[13] Thus, for example, base metals and wood and paper products, which are important items of domestic production, receive little weight in the index because they are relatively unimportant imports. The procedure adopted in calculat-ing the desired index of domestic prices was to take the group price indexes from the index of domestic wholesale prices and weight each with the import weight for that group.[14] This gives us the second component of the price variable, the relevant measure of domestic prices (P_D) for each year of the 1926–38 period.

The tariff adjustment factor is the third component of the price variable. The method of calculating this adjustment in each year and of incorporating it in the time series for relative prices of imports is described in Appendix G.

This completes the discussion concerning the derivation of the various time series re-quired for the regression analysis for current account debits. The data are given in Table XI.

Notes

CHAPTER ONE

1 We are assuming that all external transactions are classified as being either on current account or on capital account. This implies that transactions which involve monetary gold or foreign exchange reserves are included as items in the capital account rather than being shown in a special section of the international accounts.

2 Some of A's exports may be of inferior goods, but we are here concerned with her aggregate exports of goods and services. It is improbable that her exports as a whole would be inferior goods.

3 It will probably also bring about a decline in domestic investment in A; this point is discussed below.

4 The Canadian economy in the period 1926–38 had the characteristics of a dependent resource economy, as will be shown in Chapter 2 of this study. Other economies which would seem to fall into the same category are, for example, Australia, New Zealand, South Africa, and some of the countries of South America.

5 If the ratio of investment relative to national income in A is greater than in B, as it would be in a period of prosperity, such a ratio can be maintained without recourse to B only if the average propensity to save in A exceeds that in B by at least as much as the ratio of investment to income in A exceeds that in B. Since there is reason to expect the latter ratio to be higher in A than in B whereas there is no reason to expect the former ratio to differ in the two countries, it is to be expected that some part of investment in A will be financed by borrowing from B.

6 The more important are fixed money costs the greater will be the decline in profits. But even though average costs fall as rapidly as do prices (an improbable situation), there will be a fall in profits because of the fall in the volume of production.

7 Initially the effect of a slump in B may be to increase the size of A's passive current account balance. This comes about because A's exports fall whereas capital projects under construction require more time for their completion. Thus imports caused, both directly and indirectly, by the capital investment in A will be likely to fall less rapidly than will exports. The increased passive balance may require an increased rate of borrowing from B or it may be financed in some cases by a reduction in A's holdings of foreign exchange. This is purely a phenomenon of the period of transition from prosperity to recession and need not receive more detailed consideration at this stage.

CHAPTER TWO

1 Canada, Dominion Bureau of Statistics, *The Canadian Balance of International Payments, 1926 to 1948* (Ottawa, 1949), Tables III and VII, 154 and 158.

2 Canada, Dominion Bureau of Statistics, *National Accounts, Income and Expenditures, 1926 to 1956* (Ottawa, 1958), Table 2, p. 32 and also p. 26 where the percentage figures are given for each year of the period. Although, on the average, current account credits and current account debits were nearly equal for the four years shown in Table I (and also for the entire period), there were very considerable differences in individual years. In 1930 imports exceeded exports by about 30 per cent and in 1936 exports exceeded imports by 20 per cent. In other years the proportions varied within these limits.

3 *Ibid.,* Table 2, p. 32.

4 The Economic Council of Canada also draws attention to this characteristic of the Canadian economy in its *First Annual Review* (Ottawa, 1964). The "heavy dependence of the domestic economy upon international trade" is mentioned there and the statement made (p. 78) that merchandise exports "have traditionally accounted for around 50 per cent of the output of the goods-producing industries in Canada."

5 It is obvious that, for the world as a whole, current account credits are identically equal to total current account debits, so if we consider the former it is not necessary to consider the latter.

6 See the latter part of Appendix B for further details on this point.

7 This statement would be true except in cases where new discoveries more than kept pace with the exploitation of known resources. In fact, the major new discoveries of resources, notably oil in Alberta and iron ore in northern Quebec, were made in the general areas where it was confidently expected such deposits existed. In the circumstances the specific discoveries merely confirmed the previous assumptions. Discoveries of this nature may be contrasted with the fortuitous discovery of large mineral deposits in northern Ontario during railroad construction there in the first decade of this century.

8 See, for example, the topics considered in books which deal with natural resources; e.g., E. W. Zimmerman, *World Resources and Industries* (New York, 1933).

9 Atomic energy as an economic source of power was not developed until some years after the end of the period with which we are concerned.

10 Data are not given for Canada separately from Newfoundland although throughout the period 1926–38 they were separate countries. In the two cases, waterpower and iron ore, where Newfoundland had important resources, the gap between Canada and Newfoundland and the country next in order is so great that the ranking would probably be no different if per capita figures for Canada were given separately.

11 These are the major metals shown in the United Nations *Statistical Yearbook*. The others, which seem less important, are manganese, chrome, molybdenum, vanadium, tungsten, antimony, mercury, and silver. The ones we have taken to be most important are those so considered by Zimmermann, *World Resources and Industries,* Chs. XXXIV–XXXV.

12 These are also the forest products for which statistics are given in the United Nations *Statistical Yearbook*.

13 Data are not available for most commodities for 1929, and 1937 was used as the most prosperous year of the 1926–38 period, for which there are adequate statistics.

14 Although Canada does not produce bauxite, the presence of cheap and abundant hydro-electric power has made it possible for her to become one of the leading countries in the processing of this ore.

15 The fact that 1955 was a year which approached full employment while in 1937 there was substantial unemployment and production was below capacity accounts for some, but for most products only a relatively small part, of the increase in output between these two dates.

16 William C. Hood and A. Scott, *Output, Labour and Capital in the Canadian Economy*, a study prepared for the Royal Commission on Canada's Economic Prospects (Ottawa, 1957), Ch. 6, Appendix B, 437.

17 The value at constant prices of the capital stock of two other sectors related to the exploitation of natural resources, agriculture, and primary manufacturing, also increased in every year of the period 1946–55 (*Ibid.,* 435, 439). In the case of agriculture the value of the capital stock, at constant prices, more than doubled during this period; the increase for the primary manufacturing industry was 37 per cent.

CHAPTER THREE

1 This is not to deny the harmful effects of unemployment on the individual, but to deal with such considerations would take us into a broader field than the present study attempts to cover.

2 This statement is subject to qualification because of the imperfection of the index numbers on which the required calculations are based. The error from this source is likely to be small in relation to the total amount of unemployment which is being measured.

3 Many of the points which have been discussed here are also considered in Arthur M. Okun's article "Potential GNP: Its Measurement and Significance," *Proceedings of the American Statistical Association* (1962), 98–104.

4 These figures have been calculated from data in Dominion Bureau of Statistics, *National Accounts, Income and Expenditure, 1926 to 1956* (Ottawa, 1958), 32. This source is cited hereafter as *National Accounts*.

5 It is true that, in the long run, the relationship between the amount of labour employed and the amount of capital employed may be one either of complementarity or of substitutability. In the present case, in which the major changes considered are cyclical in nature, there can be little doubt that the relationship of complementarity is the dominant one.

6 This study is concerned with the effects of a deficiency of total demand. Consequently, both structural unemployment and the unemployment of some types of factors which arise from a shortage of the necessary complementary factors is irrelevant in the present context. Cf. United Nations, *National and International Measures for Full Employment* (Lake Success, 1949), 11.

7 For further evidence on this point see Appendix D, especially Table xxv.

E*

8 This figure is substantially below the factor of three which Okun found to apply to the United States in the 1950s. But, as Okun makes clear, "Potential GNP: Its Measurement and Significance," 104, he would expect the factor to be lower in a severe depression.

9 The realized average annual increase in productivity per capita during the period 1929–60 was between 1·9 and 2·0 per cent as calculated from the data in *National Accounts*. Hood and Scott *Output, Labour and Capital*, 215–21, use 2·5 per cent per man-hour per year as their lower estimate and 3·25 per cent as their upper estimate for productivity increase in the business sector; for the government and community services sector they assume continuing stability. A weighted average of these figures, adjusted from a man-hour to a man-year basis, i.e., to take into account the secular decline in hours worked per week, to make the results comparable with the figures used here, gives approximately 2 per cent as the average annual rate of per capita increase in productivity.

10 The fact that per capita productivity increased more rapidly in the highly prosperous postwar years up to the end of 1957 than it did in the less prosperous years 1958 to 1961 lends further support to this argument.

CHAPTER FOUR

1 Because Canada's exports to the United States were a large proportion of her total exports, this analysis is by no means an independent test of the original hypothesis, but it does provide a useful supplement to the material presented in this chapter.

2 In order to explain the volume of exports we must consider not only the demand for them, but also the willingness and ability of Canadian exporters to supply them under the varying conditions of the period.

3 J. R. N. Stone, *The Measurement of Consumers' Expenditure and Behaviour in the United Kingdom, 1920–38*, Vol. 1 (Cambridge, 1954), 306.

4 League of Nations, *Commercial Policy in the Interwar Period* (Geneva, 1942), 139.

5 It is probable that such cost changes in Canada will have effects, indirectly, on the other explanatory variables. These effects are likely to be slight relative to the initial disturbance under consideration and, in any case, they will be felt only after some time has elapsed.

6 The econometric technique used in deriving this equation was that of ordinary least squares. The justification for using this technique is considered in Appendix A.

7 For the number of degrees of freedom we have in this equation, a von Neumann ratio of less than 1·21 indicates the presence of positive serial correlation in the residuals (at the 0·05 confidence level). A ratio of 3·19 or higher suggests negative serial correlation, also at the 0·05 level. (See *Annals of Mathematical Statistics*, Vol. 12, 446.)

8 The regression calculated from the year-to-year percentage differences, rather than from the absolute differences, for the four variables gave the following equation:

$$X = 1·9\% + 1·36Y - 0·49P + 0·48C.$$
$$ (0·20) \quad (0·44) \quad (0·28)$$

The standard error of estimate is 2·6 per cent. The corrected coefficient of multiple correlation is 0·965 and the von Neumann ratio is 2·81. An evaluation of these results would lead to conclusions very similar to those reported in the text.

9 V. W. Malach, *International Cycles and Canada's Balance of Payments, 1921–33*, Vol. I in *Canadian Studies in Economics*, ed. V. W. Bladen (Toronto, 1954), 47. If, for example, a country's exports were principally industrial raw materials, it could be that changes in the major industrial countries would cause a change in exports from the raw material country so timed that such exports would precede the associated changes in national incomes of the importing countries.

10 League of Nations, *World Economic Survey 1937/38* (Geneva, 1938), Ch. 1 and 118–23. Note especially the reference to "speculative purchases of raw materials in the early months of 1937", p. 118. See also R. A. Gordon, *Business Fluctuations*, 2nd ed. (New York, 1961), 439–40.

11 The sum of the squared deviations of the computed values from the actual values in 1937 and 1938 is approximately 70 per cent of the total for the entire period.

12 The regression equation calculated from the percentage first differences is:

$$X = 1.8\% + 1.36Y - 0.16P + 0.47C.$$
$$\quad\quad (0.12)\quad (0.33)\quad (0.18)$$

The standard error of estimate is 1·72 per cent. The value of $\bar{R}$ is 0·983 and the von Neumann ratio is 3·23. Again our conclusions would not be materially different if they were based on these calculations rather than on the ones presented in the text.

CHAPTER FIVE

1 The principal difference between the two relates to assumptions concerning conditions of supply. In Chapter 4, when we were considering Canadian exports, it was not plausible to assume that supply was perfectly elastic and so it was appropriate to include a cost term in the regression. However, when we are considering imports into Canada it is reasonable, as a first approximation to reality, to assume that the supply of goods and services to Canada is perfectly elastic because Canadian demand (and changes in it) is a small fraction of total world demand (and changes in it).

2 For a detailed discussion of this question see D. W. Slater, "The Growth and Structure of Canadian Imports 1926–55" (unpublished PH.D. thesis, University of Chicago, 1957).

3 The computed relationship would not be disturbed if variations in the *composition* of aggregate expenditure were closely correlated with changes in the *level* of expenditure. Examination of the composition of outlay suggests, however, that there was not the close correlation required.

4 A regression based on the year-to-year percentage differences in the respective variables gave the following equation:

$$M = -0.92\% + 1.26Y - 0.80P.$$
$$\quad\quad (0.16)\quad (0.51)$$

The standard error of estimate is 3·9%, $R^2 = 0.891$ and is significant at the 0·001 level, and $\bar{R} = 0.931$. The von Neumann ratio is 1·90. Appraisal of these results would lead to substantially the same conclusions as those in the text.

5 In his study of imports made for the Royal Commission on Canada's Economic Prospects, Slater found that actual commodity imports in the late 1920s were higher than the figures given by his regression equation. See *Canada's Imports*, 88–92.

6 The advantages are not all on the side of disaggregation. It not only involves a great deal more computation but in many cases the data for the disaggregated basis are less satisfactory. For example, the adjustments required to convert the commodity trade figures to balance of payments figures are available only in aggregate, and when disaggregation is undertaken these adjustments must be allocated among the subtotals on an arbitrary basis. In general, too, more adequate price indexes are available for the aggregates. For a more theoretical analysis of the statistical aspects and some of the limitations of disaggregation, see Y. Grunfeld and Z. Griliches, "Is Aggregation Necessarily Bad?" *Review of Economics and Statistics* (February 1960), 1–13.

7 The reduction is 24 per cent and it could well have been greater except that the original figure is low and so leaves little opportunity for further reduction. In addition the data for some of the individual disaggregated equations were subject to more serious margins of error than was the case for the aggregate equation.

CHAPTER SIX

1 For further discussion of this question see *National Accounts*, 152–5.

2 Calculated from data in *National Accounts*, 32, Tables 1 and 2.

3 G. Haberler, *Prosperity and Depression*, 3rd ed. (Lake Success, 1946), 293–6.

4 The fact that the various broad aggregates which make up the GNE are classified boldly as induced or autonomous should not be taken to mean that any of these components falls entirely into one of these two categories. Consumption expenditure, for example, is classed as induced but not all consumption is dependent on the level of income; similarly domestic investment is taken to be autonomous, but it is generally agreed that some investment depends upon the level of income or upon changes in the level of income, as the voluminous literature on the acceleration principle makes clear. In short, a component of expenditure is classed as autonomous or induced on the ground that it seems generally to fit better into one of these categories than into the other. The initial basis for such a classification is that it seems not unreasonable. The final justification can be made only if the use of any given classification permits us to obtain results which are economically meaningful.

5 A similar regression equation based on the percentage, rather than the absolute, differences was also computed. The equation for this case is:

$$Y_t = -0.30\% + 0.42X_t + 0.38X_{t-1}.$$
$$\quad\quad\quad\quad (0.13)\quad (0.14)$$

The standard error of estimate is 3.5%, $R^2 = 0.823$, and $\bar{R} = 0.883$. This equation also gives a good fit to the data. The comments in the text would apply equally well to this regression, but the one based on the simple first differences is, in general, slightly preferable.

6 The total effect on income is less than the sum of the coefficients of the export variable in the two periods. For some discussion of this point and the relevant formula for the adjustment, see J. J. Polak, *An International Economic System* (Chicago, 1953), 70.

7 In the multiple regression in Chapter 5 the income coefficient was found to be 0·36. If we use a simple regression, omitting the price term, the coefficient of the income term is 0·38.

8 An alternative, and more realistic, assumption would be that induced domestic investment was approximately equal to domestic saving, but this interpretation still leaves virtually no room for autonomous investment.

9 We have excluded changes in inventories on farms from our measure of income here as we did in Chapter 5. In both cases it is preferable to consider the expenditure on farm products as being made (and the income received) when the produce is sold rather than when it is added to farm inventories.

10 An adjustment for changes in the terms of trade is necessary (for reasons explained more fully in Appendix I).

11 This question is considered at length in Appendix A of the study by M. Friedman and D. Meiselman, "The Relative Stability of Monetary Velocity and the Investment Multiplier in the United States 1897–1958" (University of Chicago, 1960). These authors use the net deficit of governments as the autonomous variable from the government sector after an extensive analysis and a number of statistical tests. It is recognized here, as it is by these authors, that, although this solution is not ideal, it is the least objectionable of the alternatives from which, in practice, our choice must be made.

12 A regression based on the year-to-year percentage differences was also computed in this case. The results are:

$$Y = -0·3\% + 0·45X + 0·20D.$$
$$(0·049)\ (0·022)$$

The standard error of estimate is 1·5%, $R^2 = 0·968$, and $\bar{R} = 0·980$. Again, as for regression II we obtain a good fit when the calculation is made on the basis of the percentage differences, but the results are not quite as good as when the ordinary first differences were used.

13 If we compute the regression from the percentage changes in these same variables the results are:

$$Y_t = -0·3\% + 0·43X_t + 0·14Y_{t-1} + 0·18D_t.$$
$$(0·038)\ (0·054)\quad (0·018)$$

The standard error of estimate is 1·0%, $R^2 = 0·984$, and $\bar{R} = 0·989$.

14 For further discussion of this point, the reader is referred to Chapter 8.

case where there are exclusions, the decision was made on the basis of *a priori* ~~rations~~ and not because better results were obtained as a result of such ex-

...nical statistical reasons we have worked with changes in these variables rather than with the original series. This is a matter of statistical technique and does not represent in principle any exception to the above statement.

3 For income in other countries, which is required in Chapter 4, we have used Colin Clark's figures from *Conditions of Economic Progress*, 3rd ed. (London, 1957). Although these have not all been deflated with a current year weighted price index, they were used because they are the best data available for the period.

4 For the aggregate regressions this occurred only in the case of the tourist and travel item. In Appendix G it was necessary to use a current year weighted index for machinery and equipment also.

5 This is a point which has also been noted by others who have investigated the experience of the Canadian economy in this period. See, for example, A. E. Safarian, *The Canadian Economy in the Great Depression* (Toronto, 1959), 8–11, 139–44.

CHAPTER EIGHT

1 *Report on the Royal Commission on Banking and Finance* (Ottawa, 1964), Ch. 23.

2 *Report of the Royal Commission on Taxation* (Ottawa, 1966), Ch. 5, 187–95.

3 The Economic Council of Canada, for example, in its *Fourth Annual Review* (Ottawa, 1967), 86, has calculated that in 1966 the actual output of the non-agricultural sectors of the Canadian economy was 99 per cent of the full employment potential.

4 *Canadian Statistical Review* (February 1968), Table 19.

5 *Ibid.*, Table 24.

6 We have placed our emphasis on the Ontario experience rather than on that of the prairie provinces because the Ontario labour force is approximately twice as large and the Ontario economy is more diversified than that of the prairie provinces.

7 For further discussion of seasonal and regional unemployment see Frank T. Denton and Sylvia Ostry, *An Analysis of Post-War Unemployment*, Staff Study No. 3 prepared for the Economic Council of Canada (Ottawa, 1964).

8 This calculation assumes that output would increase proportionately with the increase in numbers employed. This does not take into account the argument of Okun discussed in Chapter 3 which it is not appropriate to consider here since Okun's analysis applies to cyclical changes and we are concerned with structural change.

9 Our discussion has dealt with the position at full employment. But if the full employment position were improved it is reasonable to expect that the benefits would extend to other periods as well.

10 Calculated from data in Table VIII.

11 *National Accounts*, Tables 27 and 50.

12 These percentages were calculated from data in *National Accounts*, Table 5. It is interesting to note that the experience in the United States was broadly similar in this respect

to that in Canada. See A. H. Hansen, *Fiscal Policy and Business Cycles* (New York, 1941), 26.

13 Canada, Department of Trade and Commerce, *Private and Public Investment in Canada 1926–1951* (Ottawa, 1951), Table 41, 165. This calculation is based on current dollar figures, but this does not affect the general order of magnitude.

14 *National Accounts*, 1962, Table 5, p. 28. These figures, it should be noted, are in constant (1957) dollars.

15 Calculated from data in *National Accounts*, 1962.

16 *National Accounts*, 1962, 22 and *ibid.*, 1967, 15.

17 Economic Council of Canada, *First Annual Review*, 1964, 48 and *Fourth Annual Review*, 1966, 86.

18 United Nations, *Statistical Yearbook*, 1965, 560, 564.

19 For a discussion of the issues involved, see, for example, M. H. Watkins et al., *Foreign Ownership and the Structure of Canadian Industry* (Ottawa, 1968).

20 See the discussion of this question in D. A. MacIntosh, "The Cyclical Behaviour of Canada's Current Account Balance of Payments" (unpublished Master's thesis, McMaster University, 1968).

21 *Ibid.*

APPENDIX A

1 In addition to the standard textbooks and monographs which consider these topics, the empirical study by J. R. N. Stone and his associates, *The Measurement of Consumers' Expenditure and Behaviour in the United Kingdom 1920–38* (Cambridge, 1954), contains in Chapter XIX an excellent discussion of many of the questions considered in this Appendix.

2 *Econometrica*, 1960, 871. Again, in an illustrative example in his *Introduction to Econometrics* (Englewood Cliffs, N.J., 1962), 33–48, L. R. Klein assumes a one-way direction of causation in examining United Kingdom exports to the dollar area. He goes on to say (p. 49) that "for smaller and less influential countries than the United Kingdom, it would be even more legitimate to assume one-way direction of causation with or without benefit of time lags."

3 *Ibid.*

4 An alternative way of approaching this whole question would be to attempt to establish that the system of three equations could be treated as a recursive one. But this would be largely redundant in the present context and since, in addition, it would involve some rather highly technical considerations it has been omitted from the discussion. On this question, see H. Wold and L. Jureen, *Demand Analyses* (New York, 1953), 14, 49–53.

5 See, for example, the treatment of this problem in F. E. Croxton and D. J. Cowden, *Applied General Statistics*, 2nd ed. (Englewood Cliffs, N.J., 1960), Ch. 22.

6 Stone, *Measurement of Consumers' Expenditure*, 306.

7 For further discussion of this point see section 7.

8 G. H. Orcutt, "Measurement of Price Elasticities in International Trade," *Review of Economics and Statistics*, 1950, 123–5.

9 An error of constant absolute magnitude would, of course, distort the period-to-period

change if that change were measured in percentage terms. The converse argument applies when the error is of constant *relative* magnitude; in this case the absolute size of the error would vary but the percentage first differences would not be affected.

10 Klein, *Introduction to Econometrics*, 158.

11 The two methods most frequently used to deal with leads and lags are to introduce the data for the relevant periods explicitly into the equation or to determine the lag structure independently and then to use an appropriately weighted average of the data from different time periods in the final regression analysis. Either method will reduce the number of degrees of freedom in the final regression. The first of these two methods is likely also to accentuate the problem of multicollinearity and the second involves additional processing of the data before it is used in the regression analysis.

APPENDIX B

1 League of Nations, *The Network of World Trade* (Geneva, 1942). Annex I shows world trade in commodities other than newly mined gold and silver. The figures for these two products are given in Annex II.

2 League of Nations, *Review of World Trade, 1938* (Geneva, 1939), 60. The figures in this publication agree with those in *The Network of World Trade* for the years which the two publications have in common and so we can assume that the figures used for 1932 are consistent with those used for the other three years.

3 *Network of World Trade*, 15.

4 *Ibid.*, 16.

5 League of Nations, *Balances of Payments*, various years.

6 League of Nations, *Statistical Year-Book*, 1933–4, 180–1 and 1938–9, 208.

APPENDIX C

1 See the historical summary in *National Accounts*, 22–3.

2 The term *full employment* is used throughout this appendix in the sense of *full employment but not over-full employment*.

3 Royal Commission on Canada's Economic Prospects, *Final Report* (Ottawa, 1957), 329–30.

4 Bank of Canada, *Annual Report*, 1950, 3–4.

5 Dominion Bureau of Statistics, *Canada Year Book*, 1930, 738 and *ibid.*, 1932, 655.

6 Arthur M. Okun, in the *Proceedings of the American Statistical Association*, 1962, 98–104, gives the results of some calculations for the United States economy in the period after 1950 which lead to the conclusion that, in the case he was considering, a change of 1 per cent in the unemployment figure would, on the average, be associated with a change of approximately 3 per cent in real output. If we apply this factor of three to our data instead of assuming constant average returns to labour as we have done, the effect, for the "most probable" estimate, is to raise the potential full employment GNE for 1929 by 6 per cent.

For a number of reasons we have made no adjustment for this "Okun factor." It may have had a different value for Canada in the late 1920s than for the United States in the 1950s and the data available are not adequate to permit us to make an accurate estimate of it. In addition, as we shall see below, the method of estimating the full employment GNE in Canada in 1941 had to be adapted to the special circumstances of that year and it is not clear that this adjustment would be appropriate (or if appropriate how it could be made) in such circumstances.

The important point is, however, that any adjustments which we might have made for this factor (assuming it to have a value greater than one) would have had the effect of strengthening the statistical basis of the conclusion reached in Chapter 3 that the percentage unemployment approach tends to underestimate the cost of unemployment in terms of production forgone. The general contours of the shortfall of GNE would, however, have been similar to those we have calculated.

7 Calculated from *National Accounts*, Appendix, Table II, 100. The figure shown in this source is for 1 June; the average for the year would be somewhat higher.

8 General price control was not introduced until December 1941 and there was no consumer rationing until 1942.

9 The evidence suggests that output per person per year was increasing at a faster rate in the period prior to 1929 than in the years after 1929. Since these earlier years were prosperous and possibly were full employment years, it is preferable to base our estimates of a full employment income on the actual per capita GNE in each year rather than to extrapolate into this prosperous period on the basis of the depression experience. For the years between 1929 and 1941 interpolation was used.

APPENDIX D

1 The case for excluding exports of grains and farinaceous products from the figures used in Chapter 4 does not apply to the circumstances of Chapter 6 for reasons which are explained in the appropriate place in that chapter.

2 Dominion Bureau of Statistics, *Canadian Statistical Review, 1959 Supplement*, 103–4.

3 A multiple regression was also calculated in which the change in the price of wheat was included as an additional explanatory variable. The contribution of this variable to the behaviour of the dependent variable was very slight and so it was ignored in the regression mentioned in the text.

4 In 1929 the crop for each of the major grains, wheat, oats, and barley, was substantially smaller than in either the preceding or the subsequent year (DBS, *ibid.*, 108).

5 If the demand for Canadian grain products has a price elasticity of less than unity, the argument in the text would apply in the case of a *smaller* crop. The conclusion that the indirect effects of crop variations on other exports would be negligible follows in this case just as it does in the alternative case considered in the text.

6 It is worth noting here that, for the period as a whole, cash income from the sale of grains averaged about 5 per cent of GNE and the proportion did not exceed 10 per cent in any year of the period. (Calculated from data in DBS, *ibid.*, 12, 105.)

7 *Ibid.*, 109 and 112.

APPENDIX E

1 The variables X, Y, P, and C have the same meaning here as in Chapter 4 except for the exclusion of gold.

APPENDIX F

1 Because of this the two tests are not as independent of each other as might be desired.
2 Dominion Bureau of Statistics, *The Canadian Balance of International Payments, 1926 to 1948* (Ottawa, 1949), 156, 161
3 Calculated from figures given in Dominion Bureau of Statistics, *Trade of Canada* and *ibid.*

APPENDIX G*

1 The approach was modified somewhat in order to adapt it to the two special cases of interest and of dividends. Even in these cases the general form of the regression equation was retained except that for interest a simple rather than a multiple regression was used.
2 There is a minor departure from strict consistency in the cases of interest and dividends, but this is clearly justified by the nature of these items; it is not evident how the exact form of the regression equations could be preserved for these groups.
3 For two groups (machinery and equipment and tourist and travel), current year weighted indexes were used instead of base year weighted indexes in the price term. This was made necessary because we did not have the data required to compute the base year weighted price indexes.
4 The reasons for using current year weighted indexes for some variables and base year weighted indexes for others have been developed in Appendix i. The point here is simply that we should use the same type of index for a particular variable in each of our equations.
5 See, for example, H. Niesser and F. Modigliani, *National Incomes and International Trade* (Urbana, Ill., 1953), Chs. 12, 13, 14. It should be mentioned, in fairness to these authors, that they were concerned, in much of their work, with several countries and the difficulties were correspondingly multiplied.
6 For the years 1935–8 the adjustment to make the freight item consistent throughout the period has meant that the figures we have used for the balance of payments differ slightly from the published official figures.
7 The separate figures for interest and for dividends are given for the years 1926–36 in *The Canadian Balance of International Payments, a Study of Methods and Results* (Ottawa, 1939), 97–8. The 1937 and 1938 figures for dividends are available from *National Accounts*, Table 50, and the remainder of the interest and dividend item is therefore the required figure for interest. The other four service totals can be obtained directly from the balance of payments statements.

*Footnotes for Part ii of this appendix are at the bottom of the respective pages. Part ii consists of tables and explanatory notes.

8 *Canadian Balance of International Payments,* 55–8.

9 For the two groups interest and dividends it seemed preferable, *a priori,* to calculate the regression from aggregate current dollar figures rather than from per capita constant dollar figures.

10 Current year weighted price indexes were used for machinery and equipment imports and for tourist and travel because data for computing base year weighted indexes were not available.

11 In some cases it was possible to use the actual total. In others the items in a group were so numerous that it was necessary to estimate the total duties collected from a sample which would include from 80 to 95 per cent of the total gross ordinary duties.

12 For further discussion on this point see Appendix I.

13 For a study of a similar question for the Australian economy see A. T. Carmody, "The Level of the Australian Tariff: A Study in Method," *Yorkshire Bulletin* (January 1952), 52–65.

14 This procedure assumes that all changes in the proportions were the result of tariff changes. An attempt to determine separately the extent to which other factors were responsible for the change in proportions revealed that this was impossible, but it also suggested that the method we have used overstates the adjustment required, although the net effect on the price variable is very small. However, since we have not been able to deal specifically with such factors as customs administration and the tendency to impose tariff changes where the protective effect would be greatest, which had a similar cyclical pattern, the fact that the particular adjustment we have made for the price equivalent of the tariff may be overstated is preferable to having it biased in the other direction.

15 This would seem to be a reflection of the fact that protective tariffs tended to be imposed against manufactured goods rather than against imports of raw materials.

APPENDIX H

1 Dominion Bureau of Statistics, *The Canadian Balance of International Payments, 1926 to 1948* (Ottawa, 1949), 154, 158.

2 Dominion Bureau of Statistics, *The Canadian Balance of International Payments: A Study of Methods and Results* (Ottawa, 1939), 88–96.

3 Exports of grains and farinaceous products have been excluded, and it would be consistent to exclude also the freight receipts on these exports. In fact the rail freight receipts which were not included in the commodity figures were relatively small. They never exceeded $5 million and after 1929 never exceeded $2 million in any one year (*Canadian Balance of International Payments,* 85), and so no adjustment was made for them.

4 As a check on these figures an alternative calculation, based on the assumption that freight receipts would be proportional to volume of commodity exports, was made. This assumption would be invalid to the extent that Canada's exports varied during the period in the proportion handled by Canadian facilities, in composition, or in destination in a manner that would affect the relative importance of the freight item. This second calculation tended generally to confirm the results obtained by the first method.

5 The seven countries are Australia, New Zealand, South Africa, France, Germany, the Netherlands, and Japan.

6 The income data for all these countries are taken from Colin Clark, *The Conditions of Economic Progress*, 3rd ed. (London, 1957), Ch. III.

7 *Ibid.*, 142, note a. Clark's table is headed "Great Britain," but in fact the figures we use refer to the United Kingdom.

8 *Ibid.*, 18. Clark measures real income in "International units". He defined an International unit as "the quantity of goods exchangeable in the US for $1 over the average of the decade 1925–34."

9 It would be more strictly correct to adjust each country's total real income figure by its population figure, but any inaccuracy introduced by using the world population index is insignificant.

10 Dominion Bureau of Statistics, *Export and Import Price Indexes 1926–1948*, Reference Paper 5 (Ottawa, 1949). Some minor revisions to these published figures were provided by the International Trade Division of DBS.

11 For some discussion of the difficulties involved here, see H. Neisser and F. Modigliani, *National Incomes and International Trade* (Urbana, Ill., 1953), 46–9. See also J. H. Adler, E. R. Schlesinger, and E. van Westerborg, *The Pattern of United States Import Trade since 1923* (Federal Reserve Bank of New York, 1953), 69. This study deals with imports, but the same problems are involved in the choice of a price index for exports.

12 The price indices used are taken from W. A. Lewis, *World Production, Prices and Trade, 1870–1960* (Manchester School, 1952), 118.

13 For a more thorough treatment of the difficulties involved in relation to such questions, see Appendix I, where the problems of estimating the price equivalent of Canada's tariffs are discussed.

14 W. S. Woytinsky and E. S. Woytinsky, *World Commerce and Governments – Trends and Outlook* (Twentieth Century Fund, New York, 1955), 263–4.

15 Commodity imports into the US varied from a low of 39 per cent to a high of 60 per cent of all imports of goods and services into the US. The proportion was closely and positively correlated with the level of income in the US. The effect of the depression tariffs was to reduce imports of goods, but they did not affect imports of services. This is one reason for the decline in the percentage of goods in the total in depressed years. If a current year weighted index is used we give a low weight to commodities in years of high tariffs and *vice versa*. The use of a base period weighted index is an attempt to minimize this element of downward bias in the price equivalent of commercial policy.

16 For an excellent discussion of the origin, introduction, and effect on trade of the Ottawa Agreements see W. K. Hancock, *Survey of British Commonwealth Affairs, Vol. II, Economic Policy* (London, 1940).

17 Qualitative estimates of the general direction and magnitude of changes in commercial policies in the period are given in Margaret S. Gordon, *Barriers to World Trade* (New York, 1941) and League of Nations, *Commercial Policy in the Inter-war Period* (Geneva, 1942). After allowing for the special factors that apply to Canada, the general behaviour of the commercial policy adjustment factor used in this study is consistent with the trends indicated by these two more general studies of the question.

18 This argument requires qualification, however, to the extent that the *timing* of commercial policy changes differed in the United States and in other countries. Differences in timing could have significant effects over short periods, but they become less important as the length of the period we are considering increases.

19 The index we use here should exclude the tariff adjustment because we are concerned with returns to producers and not with costs to consumers.

20 Bank of Canada, *Statistical Summary, 1946 Supplement,* 107.

APPENDIX I

1 For commodity trade, the balance of payments figures, rather than those in the *Trade of Canada,* were used. For a discussion of the differences between these two figures see *The Canadian Balance of International Payments, 1926 to 1948* (Ottawa, 1949), 104–7. The basis of calculating the freight and shipping figure in the balance of payments was changed in 1935 as explained in Appendix H. In order to maintain consistency throughout the period, the figures for 1935 and later years were adjusted to make them comparable with the figures for earlier years.

2 The mechanics of deflation are different, but the end result is no different from that which would be obtained if the current dollar figure were deflated with a price index computed with current year weights.

3 These indexes were provided respectively by the International Trade Division and the Research and Development Division of the DBS.

4 *National Accounts,* 36. It will be noted that the procedure used in calculating these constant dollar figures is equivalent to deflating to current dollar series with a current year weighted price index. See *ibid.,* Table 6, n. 1 on this point.

5 On the general question of the treatment of changes in inventories on farms see the exchange between C. L. Barber and S. A. Goldberg in *Canadian Journal of Economics and Political Science,* 15 (1948), 228–30 and 541. It seems apparent from this exchange that, for our present purposes, changes in inventories on farms should be omitted from the income variable.

6 Either of these procedures involves the assumption that future prices are unchanged compared with present prices. This is the only practicable course since we know neither when the balance will be spent nor what future prices will be.

7 For further discussion of this point see R. G. D. Allen, "Index Numbers of Volume and Prices" in *International Trade Statistics,* ed. R. G. D. Allen and J. E. Ely (New York, 1953), 207–11.

8 On this matter in general, see G. Orcutt, "Measurement of Price Elasticities in International Trade" in *Review of Economics and Statistics* (May, 1950), 117–32.

9 Dominion Bureau of Statistics, *Export and Import Price Indexes, 1926–48,* Reference Paper 5 (Ottawa, 1949). Some further details and minor revisions in the published figures were provided by the International Trade Division of DBS.

10 An index so computed can be regarded as a base period weighted index if we consider each of the three components of the freight and shipping index and the price index for tourist and travel expenditures as single items. Although this is not strictly true, it

seems the best solution possible in the circumstances and is unlikely to introduce perceptible distortion into the total index.

11 On this point see the discussion in H. Neisser and F. Modigliani, *National Incomes and International Trade*, 46–9. These authors mention several possible price ratios that might be used and make clear the impossibility of choosing any one that is ideal in all respects. See also J. H. Adler, E. R. Schlesinger, and E. van Westerborg, *The Pattern of United States Import Trade since 1923* (Federal Reserve Board, 1952), who use the unweighted mean of three price indexes and explicitly recognize the impossibility of establishing that any one answer is the correct one.

12 A. C. Harberger, "The United States Demand for Imports," *American Economic Review* (May 1953), 151, n. 2.

13 This is one of the three domestic price indexes used in the Federal Reserve study.

14 It would be desirable to include service items in the index as well, particularly domestic freight and shipping, and tourist and travel price indexes. The practical difficulties of including such items in the absence of suitable domestic price indexes are, however, such that it is preferable to confine this part of the price variable to commodities only.

Bibliography

ADLER, J. H., E. R. SCHLESINGER, and E. VAN WESTERBORG. *The Pattern of United States Import Trade since 1923* (New York: Federal Reserve Bank of New York, 1952)

ALLAN, R. G. D. "Index Numbers of Volume and Price" in *International Trade Statistics*, ed. R. G. D. Allen and J. E. Ely (New York: John Wiley and Sons, 1953)

BANK OF CANADA. *Annual Report,* various years

BANK OF CANADA. *Statistical Summary, Supplement,* various years (Ottawa: Bank of Canada)

BARBER, C. L. "The Concept of Disposable Income," *Canadian Journal of Economics and Political Science,* 15 (1949)

BREWIS, T. N., ed. *Growth and the Canadian Economy.* Carleton Library No. 39 (Toronto: McClelland & Stewart, 1968)

BRYCE, R. B. "Effects on Canada of Industrial Fluctuations in the United States," *Canadian Journal of Economics and Political Science,* v (1939)

CANADA, DEPARTMENT OF TRADE AND COMMERCE. *Private and Public Investment in Canada 1926–1951* (Ottawa: King's Printer, 1951)

CANADA, DOMINION BUREAU OF STATISTICS. *Canada Year Book,* various years (Ottawa: King's Printer)

CANADA, DOMINION BUREAU OF STATISTICS. *The Canadian Balance of International Payments, A Compendium of Statistics from 1946 to 1965* (Ottawa: Queen's Printer, 1967)

CANADA, DOMINION BUREAU OF STATISTICS. *The Canadian Balance of International Payments, A Study in Methods and Results* (Ottawa: King's Printer, 1939)

CANADA, DOMINION BUREAU OF STATISTICS. *The Canadian Balance of International Payments, 1926 to 1948* (Ottawa: King's Printer, 1949)

CANADA, DOMINION BUREAU OF STATISTICS. *Canadian Labour Force Estimates 1931 to 1950.* Reference Paper No. 23 (Ottawa: King's Printer, 1951)

CANADA, DOMINION BUREAU OF STATISTICS. *Export and Import Price Indexes 1926–1948.* Reference Paper No. 5 (Ottawa: King's Printer, 1949)

CANADA, DOMINION BUREAU OF STATISTICS. *National Accounts, Income and Expenditure, 1926 to 1956, 1962, and 1967* (Ottawa: Queen's Printer, 1958, 1963, and 1968)

CANADA, DOMINION BUREAU OF STATISTICS. *Prices and Price Indexes,* various years (Ottawa: King's Printer)

CANADA, DOMINION BUREAU OF STATISTICS. *Trade of Canada,* various years (Ottawa: King's Printer)

CANADA, DOMINION-PROVINCIAL CONFERENCE ON RECONSTRUCTION. *Public Investment and Capital Formation* (Ottawa: King's Printer, 1945)

CARMODY, A. T. "The Level of the Australian Tariff: A Study in Method," *Yorkshire Bulletin* (1952)

CAVES, R. E. and R. H. HOLTON. *The Canadian Economy, Prospect and Retrospect*

Harvard Economic Studies, 112 (Cambridge, Mass.: Harvard University Press, 1959)
CHANG, T. C. "A Note on Exports and the National Income in Canada," *Canadian Journal of Economics and Political Science*, 13 (1947)
CLARK, COLIN. *Conditions of Economic Progress*, 3rd ed. (London: Macmillan & Co., 1957)
COCHRANE, D. and G. H. ORCUTT. "Application of Least Squares Regression to Relations Involving Auto-correlated Error Terms," *Journal of the American Statistical Association* (1949)
DENTON, F. T. and S. OSTRY. *An Analysis of Postwar Unemployment*. Staff Study No. 3 prepared for the Economic Council of Canada (Ottawa: Queen's Printer, 1964)
ECONOMIC COUNCIL OF CANADA. *Annual Review*, 1964, 1965, 1966, and 1967 (Ottawa: Queen's Printer)
ELLIOTT, G. A. *Tariff Procedures and Trade Barriers* (Toronto: University of Toronto Press, 1954)
FRIEDMAN, M. and D. MEISELMAN. *The Relative Stability of Monetary Velocity and the Investment Multiplier in the United States 1897–1958* (Chicago: Dept. of Economics, University of Chicago, 1960)
GOLDBERG, S. A. "The Concept of Disposable Income: A Reply," *Canadian Journal of Economics and Political Science*, 15 (1949)
GORDON, MARGARET S. *Barriers to World Trade* (New York: Macmillan, 1941)
GRUNFELD, Y., and Z. GRILICHES. "Is Aggregation Necessarily Bad?" *Review of Economics and Statistics* (1960)
HAAVELMO, T. "Multiplier Effects of a Balanced Budget," *Econometrica*, 13 (1945)
HANCOCK, W. K. *Survey of British Commonwealth Affairs. Volume II. Economic Policy* (London: Oxford University Press, 1940)
HARBERGER, A. C. "The United States Demand for Imports," *American Economic Review* (1953)
HOOD, WILLIAM C. and A. SCOTT. *Output, Labour, and Capital in the Canadian Economy* (Ottawa: Queen's Printer, 1957)
INNIS, H. A. and A. F. W. PLUMPTRE, eds. *The Canadian Economy and Its Problems* (Toronto: Canadian Institute of International Affairs, 1933)
LEAGUE OF NATIONS. *Balances of Payments*, various years. (Geneva: League of Nations)
LEAGUE OF NATIONS. *Commercial Policy in the Inter-war Period* (Geneva: League of Nations, 1942)
LEAGUE OF NATIONS. *Economic Stability in the Postwar World. Report of Delegation on Economic Depressions, Part II* (Geneva: League of Nations, 1945)
LEAGUE OF NATIONS. *The Network of World Trade* (Geneva: League of Nations, 1942)
LEAGUE OF NATIONS. *Review of World Trade*, various years (Geneva: League of Nations)
LEAGUE OF NATIONS. *World Economic Survey, 1937/38* (Geneva: League of Nations, 1938)
LEWIS, W. A. "World Production, Prices and Trade, 1870–1960." *Manchester School* (1952)
MACDOUGALL, G. D. A. *The World Dollar Problem, a study in International Economics* (London: Macmillan & Co., 1957)
MACHLUP, F. *International Trade and the National Income Multiplier* (Philadelphia: Blakiston, 1943)
MACKINTOSH, W. A. *The Economic Background of Dominion-Provincial Relations* (Ottawa: King's Printer, 1939)
MALACH, V. W. *International Cycles and Canada's Balance of Payments 1921–33. Canadian Studies in Economics* (Toronto: University of Toronto Press, 1954)

MARAIS, G. "The Influence of Cyclical Changes in National and World Income and Prices on the South African Balance of Trade between 1925 and 1939," *South African Journal of Economics* (1959)

MARCUS, E. *Canada and the International Business Cycle 1927–1939* (New York: Bookman Associates, 1954)

MCDIARMID, O. J. *Commercial Policy in the Canadian Economy* (Cambridge, Mass.: Harvard University Press, 1946)

MEADE, J. E. *The Balance of Payments, the Theory of International Economic Policy, 1* (London: Oxford University Press, 1951)

MEIER, G. M. "Economic Development and the Transfer Mechanism," *Canadian Journal of Economics and Political Science*, 19 (1953)

MUNZER, E. "Exports and National Income in Canada," *Canadian Journal of Economics and Political Science*, 11 (1945)

NEISSER, H. and F. MODIGLIANI, *National Incomes and International Trade* (Urbana: University of Illinois Press, 1953)

NEWMAN, PETER. *Studies in the Import Structure of Ceylon* (Ceylon: Government Press, 1958)

ORCUTT, G. "Measurement of Price Elasticities in International Trade," *Review of Economics and Statistics* (May 1950)

PAISH, F. W. "Bank Policy and the Balance of Payments," *Economica*, 3, New Series (1936)

PERRY, J. H. *Taxes, Tariffs and Subsidies*, 2 (Toronto: University of Toronto Press, 1955)

POLAK, J. J. *An International Economic System* (Chicago: University of Chicago Press, 1953)

POLAK, J. J. "The Foreign Trade Multiplier," *American Economic Review*, 37 (1947)

ROBINSON, T. RUSSELL. *Foreign Trade and Economic Stability*. Studies of the Royal Commission on Taxation, No. 5 (Ottawa: Queen's Printer, 1967)

ROYAL COMMISSION ON BANKING AND FINANCE. *Report* (Ottawa: Queen's Printer, 1964)

ROYAL COMMISSION ON CANADA'S ECONOMIC PROSPECTS. *Final Report* (Ottawa: Queen's Printer, 1957)

ROYAL COMMISSION ON DOMINION-PROVINCIAL RELATIONS. *Report, Book I* (Ottawa: King's Printer, 1940)

ROYAL COMMISSION ON TAXATION. *Report* (Ottawa: Queen's Printer, 1966)

SAFARIAN, A. E. *The Canadian Economy in the Great Depression*. Canadian Studies in Economics (Toronto: University of Toronto Press, 1959)

SHEARER, R. A. *Monetary Policy and the Current Account of the Balance of International Payments*. Royal Commission on Banking and Finance, Working Paper No. 9 (Ottawa: Queen's Printer, 1966)

SIMKIN, C. G. F. *The Instability of a Dependent Economy. Economic Fluctuations in New Zealand 1840–1914* (London: Oxford University Press, 1951)

SLATER, D. W. *Canada's Imports* (Ottawa: Queen's Printer, 1957)

SLATER, D. W. "The Growth and Structure of Canadian Imports 1926–55." Unpublished PH.D. thesis (University of Chicago, 1957)

SLATER, D. W. *Perspective on Canada's International Payments*. Special Study No. 3 prepared for the Economic Council of Canada (Ottawa: Queen's Printer, 1966)

STONE, J. R. N. *The Measurement of Consumers' Expenditure and Behaviour in the United Kingdom, 1920–38, 1* (Cambridge: Cambridge University Press, 1954)

STOVEL, J. A. *Canada in the World Economy. Harvard Economic Studies*, 108 (Cambridge, Mass.: Harvard University Press, 1959)

UNITED NATIONS. *National and International Measures for Full Employment* (Lake Success, N.Y.: United Nations, 1949)

UNITED NATIONS. *Statistical Yearbook*, various years (New York: United Nations)

URQUHART, M. C. and K. A. H. BUCKLEY, eds. *Historical Statistics of Canada* (Toronto: Macmillan Co. of Canada, 1965)

DE VEGH, I. "Imports and Income in the United States and Canada," *Review of Economic Statistics*, 23 (1941)

VINER, JACOB. *Canada's Balance of International Indebtedness 1900–1913* (Cambridge, Mass.: Harvard University Press, 1924)

WATKINS, M. H. et al. *Foreign Ownership and the Structure of Canadian Industry* (Ottawa: Queen's Printer, 1968)

WHITE, DEREK A. *Business Cycles in Canada.* Staff Study No. 17 prepared for the Economic Council of Canada (Ottawa: Queen's Printer, 1967)

WONNACOTT, PAUL. *The Canadian Dollar, 1948–62* (Toronto: University of Toronto Press, 1965)

WOYTINSKY, W. S. and E. S. WOYTINSKY. *World Commerce and Governments – Trends and Outlook* (New York: Twentieth Century Fund, 1955)

Index

CANADIAN STUDIES IN ECONOMICS

A series of studies now edited by Douglas G. Hartle, sponsored by the Social Science Research Council of Canada, and published with financial assistance from the Canada Council.

CANADIAN STUDIES IN ECONOMICS

A series of studies now edited by Douglas G. Hartle, sponsored by the Social Science Research Council of Canada, and published with financial assistance from the Canada Council.

1. *International Business Cycles and Canada's Balance of Payments, 1921–33* by Vernon W. Malach
2. *Capital Formation in Canada, 1896–1930* by Kenneth Buckley
3. *Natural Resources: The Economics of Conservation* by Anthony Scott
4. *The Canadian Nickel Industry* by O. W. Main
5. *Bank of Canada Operations, 1935–54* by E. P. Neufeld
6. *State Intervention and Assistance in Collective Bargaining: The Canadian Experience, 1943–1954* by H. A. Logan
7. *The Agricultural Implement Industry in Canada: A Study of Competition* by W. G. Phillips
8. *Manufacturing and Plant Location and Policy in Canada, 1946–1959* by Irving Brecher
9. *Corporate Concentration in Canada* by Gordon Blair
10. *Agriculture and the Business Cycle with Special Reference to Canada* by Clarence L. Barber
11. *The Canadian Economy in the Great Depression* by A. E. Safarian
12. *Britain's Export Trade with Canada* by G. L. Reuber
13. *The Canadian Dollar, 1948–58* by Paul Wonnacott
14. *The Logic of Dominion Taxation Structure* by Douglas G. Hartle
15. *The Demand for Canadian Imports, 1926–1955* by Murray C. Kemp
16. *The Economics of Highway Planning* by David M. Winch
17. *Economic Analysis and Combines Policy: A Study of Intervention into the Canadian Marketplace* by Stefan Stykolt
18. *The Interindustry Flow of Funds in Canada* by John F. Due
19. *Economic Growth in Canada: A Quantitative Analysis* by O. H. Firestone
20. *Capital Changes in Price Behaviour of Countries Exporting Primary Products, 1927–1958: A Comparative Study of Forty-Nine Countries* by S. G. Triantis
21. *Regional Income of Canada: Theoretic Growth* by A. G. Green
22. *International Trade and Domestic Prosperity: Canada 1926–38* by K. W. Taylor